Faith Beginnings

FAMILY NURTURING
FROM BIRTH THROUGH PRESCHOOL

by Michele E. Chronister

and Amy M. Garro

Liguori
LIGUORI, MISSOURI

Imprimi Potest:
Harry Grile, CSsR, Provincial
Denver Province, The Redemptorists

Published by Liguori Publications
Liguori, Missouri 63057

To order, call 800-325-9521
www.liguori.org

Library of Congress Cataloging-in-Publication Data

Chronister, Michele E.
  Faith beginnings : family nurturing from birth through preschool / Michele E. Chronister and Amy M. Garro.—First Edition.
    pages cm
  1. Christian education of children. 2. Christian education—Home training. 3. Catholic Church—Doctrines. I. Title.
  BV1475.3.C49 2013
  248.8'45088282—dc23
                              2013003554

p ISBN: 978-0-7648-2231-5
e ISBN: 978-0-7648-6856-6

Liguori Publications, a nonprofit corporation, is an apostolate of The Redemptorists. To learn more about The Redemptorists, visit Redemptorists.com.

Printed in the United States of America
17 16 15 14 13 / 5 4 3 2 1
First Edition

Contents

Introduction

LET THE LITTLE CHILDREN COME TO ME...

"... Jesus said, 'Let the little children come to me, and do not prevent them; the kingdom of heaven belongs to such as these'" (Matthew 19:14).

We have all heard the story of Jesus welcoming the children, and most of us would gather from this story that children are a blessing. As parents, we know this to be true—our children are, indeed, gifts!

Jesus was trying to tell us more than this, though. He taught us that we are called to make our faith like that of a child's. There is something truly profound about the faith of young children. Their faith is one of total trust in their heavenly Father, of total love for God, of genuine eagerness and curiosity to know more about God's love and mercy. The faith of a child is a gift to all who are in that little one's life.

Why Infants, Toddlers, and Preschoolers?

In recent decades, with the development of children's faith formation programs in parishes, there have been ever-increasing resources available for parents of elementary-age children to help them grow in their Catholic faith. Who do we mean by the term "younger children?" What about babies, toddlers, and the youngest of our preschoolers? What do we teach them about our faith?

These earliest years are some of the most important because they set the stage for the years to come. In these early years a child's heart and mind are open—open to whatever you choose to fill them with. Because of this, and because of their already loving and trusting nature, these littlest ones are at the perfect place to begin to know God.

It is our hope that this book will help you as you begin the faith journey with your child.

Chapter 1

FAITH BEGINNINGS IN OUR FAMILIES

Michele's Motherhood Faith Story

Growing up Catholic, I was sometimes asked if I would ever consider religious life. And I did consider it. I saw that religious life was a beautiful thing! But the more I prayed about it, I kept coming back to the fact that I felt drawn to marriage and especially to children. I had always loved working with children, whether I was babysitting or volunteering with a kids' theater camp or helping out in my mom's preschool classroom—I just loved getting to know little ones. I loved seeing how unique they each were and treating them with the respect they deserved.

I had, however, no experience with babies. The first diaper I changed was my daughter's while we were in the hospital after she was born. I knew nothing about babies and quickly realized I was in over my head. The night we brought Therese home, she wouldn't stop crying. She was tired and confused, and so was I. Still exhausted from a long labor and disoriented from my hospital stay, I couldn't stop crying, either. My husband, Andrew, took her from my arms and carried her upstairs. Awhile later she was quiet. I went upstairs and saw her sleeping on his chest, a rosary in his hands. She had fallen asleep as he whispered the prayers in her ear.

That precise moment set the tone for her faith journey with us. At every stage of life, we are discovering new ways to direct her to God and to help her know him in her own way.

I hope that what Amy and I share with you in this book will help you discover the importance of teaching faith to even the newest of arrivals: infants, toddlers, and preschoolers.

Amy's Motherhood Faith Story

John and I feel so blessed to have Charlie in our lives and another baby boy on the way. Through the years leading up to marriage, I always wanted to be a stay-at-home mom and easily pictured myself fulfilling that role. Unfortunately, despite plenty of babysitting hours, I still had quite an unrealistic picture painted in my mind of what motherhood would be like. I heard other mothers talking about how wonderful motherhood was and how exciting it was to bring a new child into the world—these things are certainly true. Still, no one mentioned how hard it could be.

Being a mother is a constant adjustment for me—mainly because my child is constantly changing. I'm often playing a game of catch-up as I struggle to understand his latest phase. Then there are the gloriously joyful times when he does something that just melts my heart, like saying a first word and giving kisses to Eeyore. Oftentimes these moments happen far apart from the frustrating struggles, so it can be challenging to keep everything in perspective. In the midst of our daily struggles, faith and family play a crucial role.

Both faith and family fuel me when I'm between those joyful milestones and in the throes of a (seemingly) week-long temper tantrum. My husband, with whom I am able to share these moments, is truly a source of great strength for me. The faith-filled moments we share as a family act as a foundation for our relationship with each other and our children. Setting aside time specifically centered on our Catholic faith help me remember what the day is really about.

In this book, Michele and I talk about how to create these faith-based moments for your own family. Different things work for different people, and by drawing both on our own experiences and those that we've heard about from other mothers, we provide you with concrete ideas to get started. Parenting can be hard—but with the right tools, parenthood is very rewarding. We hope the methods, examples, and activities we put forth in this book help you to find great joy in parenting, even during those difficult moments.

Chapter 2

PRAYER IN THE HOME

The phrase "the domestic church" is often used to describe the role of the family in the Church. In the heart of the home is Christ, experienced through the love that parents, spouses, and children give one another. In this chapter, we will discuss many elements of your family's prayer life, but before diving in, it helps to first consider what role faith plays in the home.

Little ones learn about the faith in a very different way than older children do. Little ones learn relationally and through their senses. Infants, toddlers, and even young preschoolers learn by observing the world around them. So it follows that, as parents, we naturally try to expose our littlest ones to those things that we want them to learn. We fill their rooms with colorful toys, take them for walks in the park, tell them the names of the things they point to, fill their shelves with books, and cradle them close to us. Through these experiences, they come to know much about the world; they learn practical knowledge, the beginnings of academic knowledge, and even social conventions.

Most importantly, they learn love. They learn that they are cherished, wanted, respected, and treasured. They learn what it is to be loved and what it is to love. For love is the very foundation of faith life in the home.

How can parents best help their littlest children grow in

faith? By surrounding a small child with love and affection, she grows up understanding that she is loved. And the teaching that she is loved by God is a credible one because she has already experienced God's love at work in the tenderness of her parents. In the *General Directory for Catechesis*, we learn what catechesis should consist of for infants and children. Most notably, in the description of catechesis for infants, the importance of trust is highlighted. Much of the catechesis of young childhood consists of laying the foundation of love and trust, upon which will be built an understanding and living out of the faith.

How can parents create a culture of faith in their home that will appeal to their littlest ones? Putting religious images (icons, other pictures of saints, crucifixes) on the walls will serve as little windows to heaven in your home. These images remind us of God's infinite love for us and the love we are called to give him and each other in return. Taking time to attend Mass each week as a family—and making Sunday a day to be together and rest, if possible—helps children to stay in touch with the liturgical rhythm within the context of family life. Let prayer be a normal, natural part of the day—starting the day with a morning offering. A simple prayer is enough. For example, each morning the Chronister family prays, "Loving God we offer you this day, all we think, do and say. May it be pleasing in your sight. Amen." Praying before meals and a brief family prayer at night give little ones a sense that prayer is a part of the very rhythm of their existence. So prayer becomes as normal and natural as breathing.

As with all aspects of infancy and early childhood, this time is devoted to laying foundations for what is to come. The focus is less on "learning" and more on "immersing."

Immerse your littlest ones in all that you can in regards to faith, and trust that through this exposure they are learning much about the faith. Do not underestimate the work of the Holy Spirit in their little hearts.

The Prayers of a Little One

Can an infant or even a young child pray? How can someone too young to talk or think logically have a prayer life? Many parents find themselves faced with these questions when wondering how to pray with their littlest children.

It's helpful to consider the breadth of prayer. Think about your own (adult) experience of praying. Your prayer may consist of traditional Catholic prayers, such as the Hail Mary and Our Father. Maybe you practice *Lectio Divina* by reading and reflecting on the Scriptures or other spiritual texts. Or perhaps you talk to God in an informal way, asking for what you need, or offering thanksgiving and praise. You may pray aloud or in the silence of your heart. You may be alone or in a group. Your prayer may take place in a simple environment such as your home, or a sacred place, such as a church or chapel. You might look on icons or religious artwork to direct your thoughts. Possibly you have a specific time set aside to pray, or you may be offering your prayers on the go, while at work or running errands. Prayer can take on many forms.

This more complex mode of prayer is, undoubtedly, not one you came to overnight. Most likely, it grew over the course of years as the Holy Spirit was drawing you deeper into a life of faith. The Holy Spirit is always active in our lives, particularly through our baptism. The people you have encountered in your life are gifts from the Spirit as well—your priest, teachers and professors, parents, and friends.

Creating space for the Holy Spirit to move in the life of our children is essential to their faith development. And as parents we are called by the Church to nurture the prayer lives of our young ones, who learn to pray by watching us pray.

Teaching your child how to pray is much like feeding your child. When she is born, she cannot eat anything other than her mother's milk (or a bottle, lovingly provided). She is tiny and needs constant nourishment but cannot get this nourishment by her own means—it must be provided. Gradually, she grows stronger and can participate more and more actively in the eating process. When ready, you introduce solids to your child—but not all at once. Rather, you start your child only on one food that is easy enough for her to digest and progressively add new foods to her diet. By encouraging your child to taste a large variety of foods, you will help her future diet to be more varied. She practices holding on to the spoon even before she can successfully use it to bring food to her mouth, getting used to the feel of holding it in her hand. She is eventually able to chew, to use a cup, to use utensils, and decide which food to eat, and in what order. She will grow up and be able to eat the foods you eat now.

When you feed your little one, you cater to the developmental needs he has at the time. So it is with prayer. Naturally, new forms of prayer will be introduced to your child. While he will not be able to participate in many forms himself, you should expose him to a number of forms of prayer to take in and experience. He will eventually be able to say a few words of prayer (Like "Jesus," "Mary," and "Amen"); then perhaps make the sign of the cross and fold his hands, and then eventually create his own prayers and help direct prayer time.

Infant Prayer

Newborns enter into this world and have a lot to learn. The majority of this time will be spent sleeping, eating, and taking in their new surroundings. They do this in very passive ways—by looking and listening. This, too, is what their prayer life consists of—listening to Mommy and Daddy pray, gazing at icons and other religious images, listening to a hymn being sung. Singing is an excellent way to pray with your child, and it naturally tunes in to your little one's need to be soothed. Prayer time should be associated with a sense of peacefulness, so forcing your child to participate in a prayer session while hungry or tired is counterproductive. Instead, before praying with your infant, make sure he or she is well-fed, dry, and content. This will make the experience a pleasant one for both of you.

Your prayer sessions might simply involve speaking or singing some prayers while your child is calm, perhaps even while you are lulling him to sleep. Feeding sessions are an especially good time to pray with your child, since he is a captive audience and usually quite peaceful during this time.

Nightly Family Routines

Amy writes:

When Charlie was an infant, we would incorporate bedtime prayer into his sleep routine. After we changed Charlie into his pajamas and swaddled him, we would start feeding him (or simply holding him and swaying, if he did not need to eat) and begin our prayers. We would make the sign of the cross and sing the following songs: Hail Mary, Ave Maria, Our Father, *and the* Sanctus. *He may or may not have fallen asleep during these prayers, but the important thing was that he enjoyed prayer time and got used to the concept of this special time.*

In addition to structured prayer, it is important to insert prayer naturally into parts of your child's day. By referring to "God," "Jesus," and "Mary" frequently, your child will eventually come to recognize these words. You can also talk to your little one about God, perhaps while gazing at a picture of Jesus.

As your infant grows, she will become more active and less passive. She will move toward grabbing things, moving around, and trying to talk. During this stage, you should encourage your little one to hold and touch things. If your child still finds your old prayer routine enjoyable, there is no need to change what you are doing. But if your older infant is constantly reaching for things and growing frustrated with the simplicity of prayer time, modify how you pray. Provide your child with interactive objects that are prayerful in nature—a rosary, a small icon she can grasp, or a small religious doll or figure. It may seem silly now, like you are encouraging your child to play during prayer, but what you are actually encouraging is a slightly different behavior—her normal toys are off-limits during this time. This lays the foundation for prayer time being something special.

Toddler Prayer

At this age, your child will continue to want to interact in a more active way during prayer time, so it is great to continue encouraging your child to hold and touch things like rosaries, icons, and prayer cards. A toddler—now capable of responding to simple verbal prompts—will be able to handle these objects with greater control, which will eventually mature into greater reverence. Because a child is beginning to verbalize at this point, you begin to "discuss" the faith with him. This is also a great time to introduce some new vocabulary, or start assigning words already learned to these objects in order to show their value. You can start teaching your child to handle prayer-time objects more carefully by telling him "no" if he throws the object, and to instead be "careful" and "gentle." Talk about how the items are "nice," "special," and "important" because they are "holy" and "good." Toddlers are proud of their blossoming vocabulary and take pride in being able to recognize and name objects. A toddler who has learned to say, "Jesus," will happily play the "Point to Jesus!" game whenever you spot a crucifix.

Michele writes:

I remember when Therese was beginning to recognize pictures of Jesus and would joyfully shout, "Jee! Jee!" whenever she saw a picture of him. Sometimes we would ask her to find a picture of Jesus and she would enjoy the challenge of looking around to find a picture of him and then proudly point at it. Sometimes we combined other relational skills to help her grow in a relationship with "Jee." She loved to blow kisses and so we would sometimes ask her to say bye to Jesus and blow him a kiss, when we were leaving church. She liked blowing kisses to "Jee" in the tabernacle.

Toddlers love to copy the actions of the adults around them. When you see that your child has started the mimicking game, you can work on teaching her basic actions, such as folding her hands in prayer, making the sign of the cross, genuflecting, and kneeling. The best way to teach these actions is to do them often, slowly and clearly, in front of her, and then be sure to gently correct the way she does them if necessary. When demonstrating, think about how you make the sign of the cross and slow it down. When praying, look down reverently, or look upon an icon or crucifix. Your toddler will soon learn to do the same.

Finally, remember to tap in to the wealth of traditional prayers found in the Church. From the "Hail Mary," to the "Our Father," the "Glory Be," and many others, the Church offers many beautiful prayers (all wonderful prayers to begin teaching toddlers!). This needn't be a first lesson in memorization—rather, let the prayers be learned naturally, over time, as you pray them together. You may also wish to pray informally, in your own words with your child, too. This teaches your little one that prayer is an opportunity to approach God as our Father—one who truly cares about our needs.

Michele writes:

Prayer time with toddlers is both rewarding and demanding. On the one hand, I can begin to see the results of months, and months, and months of praying with Therese—she now folds her hands when she wants us to pray, she is beginning to attempt the sign of the cross, and she recognizes images of Jesus. On the other hand, her attention span is short and her desire to wiggle is great, so we're learning to be patient with her when we pray. If we are praying together as a family, we only pray for short amounts of time together. If we are at Mass, adoration, or Stations of the Cross, we help her to tune in to significant moments and provide her with books and toys related to the faith in order to help her stay focused in her own small way. Still, she may struggle, and so we remind ourselves that ultimately it is important to teach her about God's love by loving her and being patient and understanding with her as she learns how to practice her faith.

Preschooler Prayer

The preschool child is beginning to master simple gestures (such as the sign of the cross), body postures (such as genuflecting and kneeling), and prayers. What was a great challenge as a toddler can now be accomplished with more ease. Prayer time has hopefully developed some routine, and the child should know what to expect when it begins. By repeating some of the same traditional prayers each day, she will be able to pick up on them and hopefully start saying them along with you. If she does not start doing this on her own, but can talk well, try practicing them outside of prayer time. Say one line at a time and have her repeat it back to you. Doing this once a day with a single prayer will help her learn it more quickly. Encourage her to join in the parts she remembers during family prayer time. You are working toward a higher level of participation at this age.

Continuity and devotion to certain prayers will offer her stability and help her to learn them more quickly. Small children thrive on repetition and predictability! Because you want prayer time to be a time when your child feels a sense of security, it is important to make the family prayer routine consistent and predictable. There may be variations—as on special feast days or liturgical seasons—but there should also be some common features to this time together. Consider choosing a few prayers that will remain the same, rotating in different prayers on occasion.

This is also an age that appreciates active participation in family prayer, as well as including informal prayer. Preschoolers love an opportunity to offer petitions! They also love listing the things for which they wish to thank God. You can prompt your child with questions, such as, "What would you like to thank God for today?" or, "Who would you like to pray for at this moment?" Preschoolers love to be included in prayer in this way.

> *Michele writes:*
>
> *I vividly remember prayer time with the three-year-olds when I was assisting in a Level I Catechesis of the Good Shepherd atrium. They loved the opportunity to pray for their own special intentions. Memorably, I remember such gems as a little boy asking us to pray for "cars."*

Family Prayer Corner

It is easy to get caught up in the busyness of our lives and not stop to pray. But it is always important to remember that prayer time is family time. Blessed Pope John Paul II teaches us that "family prayer has its own characteristic qualities. It is prayer offered in common, husband and wife together, parents and children together…The words with which the Lord Jesus promises His presence can be applied to the members of the Christian family in a special way: 'Again I say to you, if two of you agree on earth about anything they ask, it will be done for them by my Father in heaven. For where two or three are gathered in my name, there am I in the midst of them'" (*Familiaris Consortio*, 59). By praying together as a family, we invite Christ into our midst, helping our littlest ones to come to know his love.

The entire mode of teaching very young children about the faith should follow this pattern. Begin by surrounding them with images, sounds, smells, etc. that relate to the faith and they will begin to make it their own. If practice of the faith is a part of the family culture, then children will find it natural to practice their faith.

Although you will have reminders of your faith scattered throughout your home (such as crucifixes in each room, or beautiful pictures of Jesus and the saints), a specific prayer corner is an invaluable addition for any family. This prayer corner can be as simple or as elaborate as you desire, but it should be a place where your family can regularly come together to pray, and where your particular flavor of piety is well-represented (for example, you may wish to include images of patron saints).

Select a corner of your home where you may have a small table or shelf and prepare it to be a place of prayer. Consider including a rosary, your family Bible (and perhaps a children's picture Bible as well), prayer books, beautiful images and icons, and maybe some holy water in a small container. Use churches, chapels, and shrines that move you as inspiration for your own prayer space. Include accessories you see at these locations to add beauty, creating an environment fit for worship. This might include things like beautiful linens, candles (placed safely away from small hands), religious statues, or even a photograph of your favorite church. For example, if you practice a devotion to Our Lady of Lourdes, consider displaying a Saint Bernadette statue and a photograph of the grotto. Be sure to use devotions, images, and objects that mean something to you—the more passionate you are about prayer time and the prayer space, the more passionate your child will be.

As a way to further engage the very young child, you may wish to also make a miniature prayer corner. This corner can be next to the family prayer area to be used during prayer time, or it might be in a separate area for her to focus on throughout the day by exploring and learning more about her very own religious objects. Using a small stool or basket, gather together religious objects and images that are important to your child (perhaps an icon of a favorite saint, a picture of Jesus that he or she likes, or a favorite Catholic picture book). The littlest of children will explore this corner with great curiosity, and as he or she grows older this will become a place of respite and quiet.

Michele writes:

In the course of writing this book I have had to relocate and modify Therese's prayer corner several times so that it could be a place that would actually engage her. What I've most recently settled on is using the shelf that is right beneath the top of the bookshelf where our family prayer table is located. One day as we were praying together, I realized that her line of sight went straight to that shelf and so it made sense to claim it for her! I arranged a children's prayer book, a few plastic statues, and a wooden icon there for her. Now, when we pray together as a family, she can look at her little shelf to help her pray.

When it comes time for your family to pray together each morning or evening, gather around this prayer corner. Let it be an ongoing reminder of Christ, who is at the heart of your home. This time in your prayer corner should be a tender and gentle time for your family. Voices should soften, children be gently embraced, and movements done with care and reverence. This space is where you will begin and end your days as a family every day. The tone you set in this space, in those times of prayer, will shape your child's days. Do your best to make the prayer space a comfortable and enjoyable place, while teaching your child reverence. She should learn to cherish this place and feel at home in it.

Family Prayer Box

Family life is filled with prayer intentions—prayers to be offered for family and friends, as well as for personal needs. It can be difficult to keep track of all of these "special intentions." One solution is the family prayer box.

A family prayer box can be as plain or as decorated as you wish. It can be a painted or unfinished wooden box or a shoebox. No matter how it looks, the family prayer box can be a place to record names or draw pictures of those for whom your family wishes to pray. Next to the prayer box, you may wish to place a stack of small pieces of paper and some crayons and pencils in order to write petitions. When your children are very small, the family prayer box will be something that the parents use—a place for them to keep track of all of the needs or intercessions for which they will pray. As children grow older, they can include their own special prayers in the prayer box. And when they are old enough to write, they can write the names of those for whom they would like to pray. Before that they can draw pictures of the people that they hold dear in prayer, or parents can write down the intentions for them.

A prayer box can be a permanent fixture in the home—something that is kept in the prayer corner, where intentions can be added at any time. Or it may be a part of the family's ritual prayer, a place where they add their special intentions together as a family at the end of the day. Either way, it can serve as a tangible reminder of the people and intentions that your family holds dear in prayer.

Learning to Pray the Rosary

The rosary can be prayed with your child from the start—even before birth! Many Catholic stores sell simple "first rosaries" for young children. However, because little ones often do not have the attention span to pray through an entire rosary, why not consider starting small? Begin by simply praying one decade of the rosary (or even the first three beads). While praying the decade or first few beads, you may wish to encourage your little one through it; she will grow accustomed to the sight and feel of a rosary, thus laying the foundation for devotion to this beautiful prayer.

There are a number of things you can do to draw your children into praying the rosary. For example, your entire family can pray the rosary in a room with a statue of Mary and have the youngest children take turns placing a flower at the foot of Mary at

Michele and Therese hold hands and embrace the rosary.

the beginning of each decade. This helps redirect and refocus your young child's attention throughout a lengthier form of prayer. Other families find rosary books that include pictures of each decade to be helpful. You may consider making or purchasing small dolls or toys that can be used to allow your young children to act out different decades as you pray them.

The rosary can be a regular prayer in your family—prayed together daily, or weekly, or monthly. It may be an occasional prayer. Feel free to pray it as frequently or infrequently as you feel called to do, but do not underestimate your family's ability to pray it together!

Michele shares:

Our family has found that the rosary can having a calming effect when nothing else can. Sometimes, when we are taking a road trip as a family and Therese is getting fussy and restless, we pray the rosary aloud and it helps her to calm down. Sometimes, listening to us pray the rosary even soothes her to sleep!

Amy shares:

The rhythmic form of the rosary is often helpful for Charlie to hear during Mass when he has trouble paying attention. It is both soothing and captivating when he is fussing and bored. One huge benefit of praying the rosary at this time is that I can still be immersed in prayer during the Mass even while attempting to engage a restless toddler. We walk around and point to various objects of interest in the church while praying in quiet whispers.

Even if your littlest ones are unable to pay attention to the rosary in the beginning, simply surrounding them with this beautiful prayer—and asking for the intercession of their heavenly Mother—can go a long way in helping them grow in their faith.

A Wealth of Prayers

There are many different forms of prayer, and many different prayer traditions. The following are some of the most basic, foundational prayers in our faith.

The Lord's Prayer (also known as the **Our Father**) holds a special place in our faith. Jesus gave us the very words to this prayer in response to the request, "Lord, teach us to pray" (Luke 11:1). Jesus teaches us to approach God as our Father, and little ones will hopefully be very familiar with the experience of asking Abba ("Daddy") to help and be with them:

> *Our Father who art in heaven,*
> *hallowed be thy name;*
> *thy kingdom come,*
> *thy will be done*
> *on earth as it is in heaven.*
> *Give us this day our daily bread,*
> *and forgive us our trespasses,*
> *as we forgive those who trespass against us;*
> *and lead us not into temptation,*
> *but deliver us from evil. Amen.*

Hail Mary

Through the Hail Mary, we ask that our mother Mary offer her loving prayers for us and for our personal needs. The Hail Mary prayer is primarily echoing the words spoken by the angel Gabriel in the Gospel of Luke. Because of her unique role as the Mother of God, Mary can intercede with her Son on our behalf, so at the end of this prayer we ask our Lady to *pray for us*. Little ones should be taught to turn to Mary with the same loving trust that they have in their own mothers, for she is our *Heavenly Mother*, ready at every moment to help us:

> *Hail Mary,*
> *Full of grace, the Lord is with you.*
> *Blessed are you among women*
> *and blessed is the fruit of your womb, Jesus.*

Holy Mary,
Mother of God, pray for us sinners,
Now and at the hour of our death.

Glory Be

The Glory Be is a simple and short prayer that is easy to memorize and beautiful in its brevity. Each time it is prayed, it is a reminder of the Holy Trinity—Father, Son, and Holy Spirit—who we are called to love with all our hearts:

Glory Be to the Father, and to the Son,
and to the Holy Spirit,
As it was in the beginning, is now and ever shall be,
world without end. Amen.

Litanies

Litanies are prayers that ask God to help us and implore the saints to pray for us. They have a few simple responses and are therefore a great prayer for children as they are developing their speech. Because they can be lengthy, you may want to shorten them for your child. For example, a shortened version of the *Litany of the Saints* could utilize one response only: "pray for us." Your preschooler can easily master this short sentence. There are a number of litanies, both private and public, that you can adapt to your family needs. You can also create your very own *Litany of the Saints* by listing off your confirmation saints or the saints of your namesake. For example, the Garro family litany might go something like this:

"Saint John the evangelist, pray for us.
 Saint Michael the archangel, pray for us.
 Saint Dominic Savio, pray for us.
 Saint Bernadette, pray for us."

Create variety in your prayer routine by including these different types of prayer:

- **Traditional** prayers (such as the ones listed above)
- **Intercessory** prayer, where you ask saints to pray for you
- **Petitions**, where you ask God's help for certain things
- **Free-form** prayer, where you simply speak your thoughts to God.

Of course, there is no need to include all of these types of prayer into one prayer time. Be sure to keep your child's attention span in mind. For example, you might say some traditional prayers and some intercessory prayers in the morning, and petitions and free-form prayer at night. Above all, make a prayer routine that works well for your family.

Activities

ACTIVITY 1: *MY FIRST PRAYER BOOK*

Many of the most beautiful and significant prayers in our faith have been passed down from generation to generation. These poignant and traditional prayers often put into words what we ourselves want to say, and many of them are deeply rooted in Scripture (the *Our Father*, the *Hail Mary*, *Magnificat*, etc.). By passing on the treasure of these prayers to your little one, you provide him or her with some useful tools that will be used many times throughout his or her prayer life.

A helpful aide in sparking their interest in these prayers is a prayer book. Prayer books are a common staple of the Church's prayer life—used to contain the daily readings (for example: **Lectionary**), the important prayers at Mass (for example: **the Roman Missal**), and to hold the cycle of prayers prayed by priests, religious, and lay people throughout the world (for example: **Liturgy of the Hours**). Giving your little ones a "first" prayer book helps them to tap in to one of the many tangible reminders of our faith. A prayer book builds up the family's Catholic culture, and by making your own you can be sure to include the prayers that are most important to your family. Simple picture prayer books can often be found at your local Catholic bookstore or can be purchased online.

You can also make you own.

You will need:

- Photo album or a binder with page protectors (smaller is better, so your child can hold it)
- Prayer cards (bought at a Catholic bookstore or printed from your computer)

Directions

1. Purchase holy cards with your favorite prayers and with pictures of your favorite saints, or print out these prayers and pictures.

2. Arrange them on the pages of a photo album or slide them into page protectors in a binder.

3. Read through your "prayer book" with your child, and even take the "prayer book" to Mass with you, to help your child when he or she is restless.

ACTIVITY 2: *INTRODUCING PRAYER CARDS AND ICONS*

Little ones have a natural sense of beauty and are easily attracted to beautiful images of saints and Jesus. Because of this, prayer cards and icons are ideal tools for teaching small children about the faith. Prayer cards and icon cards are also great for little hands to hold and carry with them.

You will need:

- Your favorite icons or religious images

Infants enjoy gazing at icons due to their colors, beauty, symmetry, and interesting new faces. When your child is old enough to grasp objects, consider giving her her very own icon. A small icon printed on a wooden block is great for small hands. Fabric icons are excellent for infants since they are soft, a tactile object that will interest or soothe them. You can easily make your child fabric icons by using iron-on paper to print and transfer some of your favorite images to white felt.

As your child grows older, you can substitute these fabric icons with laminated prayer cards (about a dollar each at your local Catholic bookstore). Punch a hole in the top, and place them on a metal ring or ribbon for your child to enjoy without fear of losing them. As your child broadens her vocabulary, teach her the names of the saints on her cards and the icons throughout the home. When your little one is able to speak in full sentences, teach her the phrase "pray for us" and incorporate intercessory prayer into your daily routine.

As your child becomes a preschooler, you can begin explaining that we pray to certain saints for special intentions. For example, you might teach your child that Saint Anthony is great to talk to when we have lost something. Give him an icon of Saint Anthony and teach him the prayer, "Tony, Tony, look around, something has been lost and must be found." Read short stories about the saints to him while he looks at an icon, or read him a story from a picture book about saints. You can lay the icon prayer cards out and ask him to tell you the stories he has learned about the saints. During prayer time, invite your child to ask his favorite saints to pray for him. Have his prayer cards available to prompt him in this endeavor.

The goal of introducing your child to icons is to help him learn about these saints and to direct his prayers and attention to holy thoughts. This will start with your child simply looking at and enjoying her beauty; she can later be guided into a deeper understanding. While it may seem like a toy now, your child can eventually be taught that it is a very special object. For very young ones, prayer cards and icons may be treated more like a toy—handled with the same sort of love and curiosity as a favorite stuffed animal. This stage of exploration has its place, as just holding and carrying these images helps open their hearts to learning more about God. Gradually, over time (and certainly by the time they reach the end of early childhood) they will learn how to treat these icons with the gentleness that they deserve.

For the Record

We blessed my bedroom on _____

We blessed our home on _____

We created our prayer corner on _____

It was filled with _____

_____

The first prayer I learned was _____

_____

FIRST YEAR

My bedtime prayers are _____

_____

_____

_____

Other prayers we say throughout the day are _____

_____

_____

During prayer time, I _____

_____

Some special memories include _____

_____

_____

_____

SECOND YEAR

My bedtime prayers are _____

_____

Other prayers we say throughout the day are _____

_____

_____

During prayer time, I _____

_____

_____

_____

My favorite prayers are _____

_____

_____

_____

My favorite thing to do in the prayer corner is _____

_____

_____

Some special memories include _____

_____

_____

_____

_____

THIRD YEAR

My bedtime prayers are _____

_____

_____

Other prayers we say throughout the day are _____

_____

_____

During prayer time, I _____

_____

_____

My favorite prayers are _____

_____

_____

Other prayers I know include _____

_____

_____

I like to ask God for _____

_____

My favorite thing to do in the prayer corner is _____

_____

_____

Some special memories include _____

_____

_____

FOURTH YEAR

My bedtime prayers are _____

_____

_____

Other prayers we say throughout the day are _____

_____

_____

During prayer time, I _____

_____

My favorite prayers are _____

_____

_____

Other prayers I know include _____

_____

_____

I like to ask God for _____

_____

My favorite thing to do in the prayer corner is _____

_____

_____

Some special memories include _____

_____

_____

Chapter 3

THE SACRAMENT OF BAPTISM

The moment a child enters the world is remarkable. The anticipation, the silence before that first cry—it is truly an unforgettable experience. Even more memorable is the moment when a child is first embraced by his or her family. The first moment the nurse lays a newborn in a mother or father's arm, or the first time a little one is placed in the arms of his or her adoptive parents...these are truly sacred moments. They are moments in which we encounter the reality of God's love for us and for our families in a tangible way.

Baptism is the Church's equivalent of those moments. As the water is poured over the child and the holy words are spoken, the child is laid in the arms of God her Father, and in the arms of mother Church. The little one is embraced by all the Church, with absolute love and joy, and forever cleansed of the stain of original sin. Surrounded by this grace, the child is more complete because he or she is loved in a way that is richer and fuller than even the parents could love him or her.

The gift of baptism is truly the greatest gift that parents can give their children. Just as they so willingly give physical life to their little one, they now willingly give the gift of spiritual life to their child. Yet, this is not just the work of the parents, but the work of God being enacted through the parents. What a beautiful gift for the mother and father to give their child—a life in God.

Two requirements are necessary in order for a child to be welcomed into the Church through baptism:

1. The parents (or at least one of the parents) must consent for the child to be baptized.

2. The parent(s) must have the child baptized with the hope that he or she will grow up faithfully in the Church.

Grounded in the hope of salvation for their child, parents enter into the process of bringing their child into the family of the Church.

What Is Baptism?

The *Catechism of the Catholic Church* defines baptism as "the basis of the whole Christian life, the gateway to life in the Spirit (*vitae spiritualis ianua*), and the door that gives access to the other sacraments. "Through Baptism we are freed from sin and reborn as sons of God; we become members of Christ, are incorporated into the Church and made sharers in her mission" (*CCC* 1213). Through our baptism, we enter fully into the spiritual life. Not only is the soul wiped clean of original sin when one is baptized, but it is also opened to the Holy Spirit. At baptism, a little one who was once an ordinary baby becomes a child of God and temple of the Holy Spirit. The child is given the gift of God's own life in his or her life.

Baptism also welcomes your child into the family of the Church, allowing him or her to become a part of the body of Christ. This is the beginning of the faith life of a child, where one becomes a full participant in the life of the Church—including the full sacramental life. Through the sacraments—beginning with baptism—the child becomes one with God and experiences his life and grace in an intimate way. The child will be able to have his or her sins forgiven (reconciliation), experience union with Christ through receiving his Body and Blood (Eucharist), receive the Holy Spirit and all gifts of the Spirit (confirmation), to be given abundant grace in his or her vocation (matrimony and holy orders), and given grace and healing in times of real suffering and ultimately at the moment of death (anointing of the sick). New parents often hear that if they do x, y, or z, they will be giving their child "the best start." This is yet another example of that. If you baptize (or have baptized) your child, you are truly giving your little one the absolute best start, as you prepare your little one for fullness of life in God.

Preparing for Baptism

Typically, you will be asked to attend a parent meeting or class to prepare you for the baptism of your child. Just as you attend an infant-care class or a childbirth class, this class prepares you to welcome your child into the world. The priest, deacon, or parish worker at your parish will help you to understand what is being asked while raising your little one in the faith, and you will have the opportunity to ask any questions that you may have. It is a gentle, welcoming experience (or at least it should be!) in which the Church shares in your joy over your newest little one. Some churches also require the godparents to attend this class preparing you for the baptism of your child. If your child's godparents are out of town, they may be able to attend a similar class at their church or a nearby church to fulfill this requirement. Often churches will also require some documentation that the godparents-to-be have been confirmed (sacrament of confirmation). (Older children can also be baptized, but for our purposes here we will primarily focus on the baptism of infants. The baptism of a toddler or very young child who has not yet reached the age of reason has a similar process.)

In addition to attending class, you may want to tell your child about his or her upcoming baptism. There are picture books about baptism; consider reading one to your child. Infants will not understand what you are saying, but it is still important to include them in the preparations in some aspect. In many ways, these preparations are more for the parents and godparents and serve to remind us of the importance of the sacrament.

A more significant form of preparation is that of prayer. Your child is about to undergo a great transformation and will receive a great blessing from God. Pray that the commitment to the Church you make on your child's behalf is one he or she will take up in the future. You may also pray that God gives you (the parents) the grace to lead him or her to the love of Christ. You may also wish to offer a novena to the Holy Spirit (which you can find using a quick online search) leading up to the baptism of your child. A novena is a nine-day prayer that follows the example of the disciples in the upper room who prayed for the coming of the Holy Spirit after Christ had ascended into heaven. Many Catholics around the world pray for special intentions using this prayer form, a beautiful prayer of preparation for your child's baptism. The future godparents of your child may also enjoy taking part in these prayer options. See the "Wealth of Prayers and Activities" section at the end of this chapter for some other prayer suggestions.

Michele writes:

Leading up to the baptism of Therese, we spent a lot of time praying with her (even though she was still a newborn and didn't understand what we were saying!). Most memorably, we spent the nine days leading up to her baptism praying a novena to the Holy Spirit, asking the Holy Spirit to fill her with God's love and grace and to enable her to become the person that God has created her to be. It built up our anticipation as parents, and I truly believe it helped our family to be open to the grace and gifts that our daughter received through baptism.

The Rite of Baptism

Just as entrance into a family is a beautiful event—surrounded with specific rituals performed in much joy (that is, the naming of the child, beginning to nurse the child at the breast or bottle, bringing him or her home from the hospital, laying the child in a crib or bassinet for the first time, changing the first diaper, giving the first bath, etc.); so, too, the Church surrounds the reception of her new children with much joy and tradition.

On the day of your child's baptism, the priest or deacon will greet your little one at the door of the church with special prayers and with some questions and answers designed to help you state your desire to have your child baptized and officially welcomed into the Church. As parents, then, you are asked to renew your baptismal vows.

The actual Rite of Baptism is a truly joyous one. As the priest or deacon anoints the child with the oil of catechumens and performs the "Ephratha" rite, he will bless the ears of the child that he or she may be open to hearing the word of God and the mouth that he or she may proclaim the gospel. As the rite continues, holy water is poured over the little one's forehead to signify God's sanctifying grace as original sin is washed away and new life given to the child. The child is anointed with fragrant chrism oil, anointed as a "priest, prophet, and king" (*CCC* 1241)...a new creation in Christ. The baptismal candle is lit from the Easter candle to illumine that Christ has enlightened the child and is a sign that the child is, through Christ, the light of the world. With great joy, the assembly welcomes the little one with applause and prayers. Your little one may be baptized during Mass, or at some other appointed time, more privately. In both situations, those in attendance represent the Church, welcoming your child with open arms into her membership.

Another symbol in baptism is the white garment that your child wears. The color white often signifies purity, a calling for the entire Church as the people of God. For baptism, the white of the garment indicates the purity of soul that all new members of the faith are given by God. During baptism, our souls are wiped clean of sin and are pure as snow, and this garment "symbolizes that the person baptized has put on Christ" (*CCC* 1243).

Amy shares:

My siblings and I all wore the same gown during our baptisms—my father's gown. I love traditions and the special meaning and sentiment that my father's gown had, so I wanted Charlie to be baptized while wearing it as well. Unfortunately, it was quite worn and too delicate to be used again. I was trying to figure out a way to make a new gar-

ment special and read about a new trend where baptismal gowns are sometimes created from the mother's wedding dress. My mother sewed a beautiful baptismal gown from some extra wedding dress fabric we had. This garment, though new, carried a special meaning behind it—a child was, in a sense, the fulfillment of our wedding vows. It was amazing to have these two sacraments linked in that way.

Many new mothers now take their wedding dresses (or extra fabric from their dress, jacket, veil, or shawl) to have made into or incorporated into a baptismal gown. You can also use a family baptismal gown or make the garment special by having a separate garment for each child. These can be custom-made, sewn by you, or found in the majority of baby stores.

At What Age Should We Baptize Our Infant?

There is no minimum age for baptism and no reason to wait to baptize your child apart from the practical. For example, it may be difficult or undesirable to baptize a two-day-old baby due to reasons such as the health of the child, establishment of new routines, and the recovery of the mother. Aside from these considerations, there is no reason to wait to baptize your child, since in the eternal sense, your child has no deeper need than to know the Lord. In fact, the Church urges prompt baptism: "Parents are obliged to take care that infants are baptized in the first few weeks; as soon as possible after the birth or even before it, they are to go to the pastor to request the sacrament for their child and to be prepared properly for it" (*Code of Canon Law* 867.1). While it is common to wait for many months to a year to baptize infants, this should not be the norm.

Amy writes about Charlie's baptism:

We scheduled Charlie's baptism six weeks after his due date. As first-time parents, we weren't sure what to expect, but we knew that women are allowed up to six weeks of absence from Mass after birth, so we felt that this was a good time to have him baptized. We figured that if I were able to attend Mass again, then there was no reason to wait longer. Charlie actually ended up coming two weeks early, but with hotel rooms reserved for out-of-town guests, a re-hospitalization, and a difficult breastfeeding relationship, we thought it unwise to move the baptism date. We were very happy with the timing and will probably schedule any future baptisms for around six weeks of age as well.

Michele writes about Therese's baptism:

Therese was baptized when she was about a month old. It ended up working out well, because she was old enough to easily be taken out of the house. I've known of people baptizing their little ones even younger, and I must admit that I was eager to get her to the waters of baptism. I felt both joy and relief when I knew she had been baptized—it was as important to her well-being as those first few appointments with her pediatrician in my mind (and I certainly wouldn't skip any of those!). It made me so happy to know that I had given her all I could in terms of both physical and spiritual health.

Depending on the timing of your child's birth in relationship to the Church seasons and holy days, you may need to choose between having a very early baptism and waiting a bit longer. For example, the Church does not normally allow baptisms during Lent. If your child's due date is just before or during Lent, you may want to ask your pastor about having your child baptized at the Easter Vigil Mass. These special liturgies provide a beautiful backdrop for such a special event. Baptisms can be performed any day of the week, but Sundays (or Saturday after the Vigil Mass) are the preferred day for baptisms (*CCL* 856).

Choosing Your Godparents

The Church instructs us that a godparent "helps the baptized person to lead a Christian life in keeping with baptism and to fulfill faithfully the obligations inherent in it" (*CCL* 872). We can see from this statement that the role of the godparent is explicitly spiritual and religious. Though they do not supersede the place of the parent as the primary educators of the faith, godparents are intended to aid parents in their endeavor to teach the faith. Practically speaking, what are the requirements for becoming a godparent? In order to be a godparent, one cannot be a parent of the child, must be at least sixteen years old (unless your local bishop has decided otherwise), and be a practicing Catholic in good standing with the Church—having received both the sacraments of Eucharist and confirmation (*CCL* 874).

Consider the important spiritual and religious roles your child's godparent(s) will play as you prepare for your child's baptism. Because the role of the godparent is spiritual and religious—not just cultural—it is important to think about their faith life. How are those whom you want to godparent your child living their faith? Will he assist your little one to grow in faith and maturity? He has the potential to influence your child. If he speaks kindly to others and about others, and he shows reverence and prudence when speaking about religious topics, this will set a good example for your child. On the other hand, if he is outspoken about his disbelief in various teachings, he may instill doubt in your child's mind. If your child were to ask this godparent about a Church teaching, do you feel confident that he would answer in a manner that challenges the child to grow faithfully alongside the entire Church?

Next ask yourself, what does this person's actions show about her faith? Does she set a good example? Keep in mind she must be living out the Catholic faith. She should attend Mass on Sundays and holy days of obligation. Regardless of how spiritual someone may seem, she must fulfill this obligation in order to be considered in good standing with the Church. It would be wonderful if she could pray with your child or take your little one to adoration. Do you think she would be comfortable doing these things with your child? Even if godparents are in a different city, they can still foster a spiritual relationship by praying for the child. No godparent relationship looks exactly the same, but it should always be faith-filled. When choosing your child's godparents, imagining what the dynamic will look like can aid your decision.

Consider what this relationship will look like through all ages and stages, as you are not simply choosing a godparent for your child as an infant, but for his entire life. In the future, what kind of interaction and connection do you envision? Do you believe this individual will fulfill that vision? How will the godparent help you or the child during difficult times, especially if your child questions some or all of his or her faith? Will this individual continue to encourage your child to live in the faith for a lifetime and to carefully discern a vocation? Will he or she set forth a good example and encourage faithfulness to the Church in teachings that many in our culture do not embrace, such as teachings on chastity? Don't discount an individual as a bad choice for a godparent simply because he is "not good with kids," for some godparents might be better to mentor your young one as he or she begins to mature. The Church advises us that it is desirable for the godparent to also be the confirmation sponsor (*CCL* 893). This, of course, is not a requirement, but it shows us the importance of the continued role of the godparent in your child's faith life.

Choosing godparents in practice frequently is likened to the choice of a best man or maid of honor. That is to say, oftentimes this choice reflects a close friendship rather than the parents' view that these individuals are good examples of the faith. But choosing a godparent is not about honoring a special friend, encouraging a close relationship between a family member and your child, or repaying a favor (such as asking someone to be your child's godparent simply because you are theirs, though if you have selected faith-filled friends, this could certainly be true). The first priority is to make sure that you, as parents, feel that your children's godparents could indeed help them to grow in their faith and fulfill their baptismal vows. This choice will hopefully be very easy, but it can be a very difficult one, especially in close families where feelings may be hurt. Just keep in mind that the choice is ultimately about your child and his or her best interest. Like any other time of discernment in your life, we suggest you approach it with careful thought and prayer.

Michele writes:

I am so grateful for Therese's godmother, who is my twin sister. Each time we visit with her, she makes a point of praying with Therese before bedtime. Recently, my husband (who normally leads us in prayer before Therese's bedtime) was out of town. We spent that time with my sister and my parents. During this time while my husband was away, my sister made a point to pray with Therese each night before bed. She is a young woman who I know has grown up surrounded by a culture of faith and I know that she is someone who Therese will be able to talk to about her faith as she gets older. I look forward to seeing them share more faith experiences together as she gets older. I am confident that they will have many moments to celebrate Mass together, learn prayers, experience first Communion, etc.

Celebrating Baptism

Your child's baptism is a very exciting day—the day he is washed clean from all sin, so a celebration is in order. Do what you feel up to with a newborn, but a family get-together and modest gifts for your child are wonderful ways to rejoice. Some gift ideas might include a crucifix, rosary, Bible, icon, or saint cards—items that commemorate this day and can be used and cherished for a lifetime. But a celebration of baptism need not happen only once, for we remember our baptism every time we go to Mass and cross ourselves with holy water and when we renew our baptismal vows at Easter. Mark baptism dates on the calendar and do something special to remember that day each year, just as you would celebrate a birthday. Cook a special meal, visit a local shrine, or attend Mass on that day; say a few prayers of thanksgiving for God's gift of the sacrament, and look at pictures of that special day. As your child grows older, help her to memorize her baptismal day just as she remembers her birthday, as they are both extremely important milestones.

Living Out the Sacrament

Now that your child is baptized, seek to continually fulfill the promise you made to raise your child in the Catholic faith. As you take to heart the rest of the suggestions in this book, be sure to incorporate your child's godparents into this process. Make a point of setting aside some quiet prayer time for your child to spend with his or her godparents when they visit, even if it is just a few moments. Invite them to participate in daily prayer and to celebrate your child's baptismal anniversary each year. In your prayer intentions, encourage or help your child to pray for his or her godparents, thanking God for their presence in your lives.

Amy shares:

The first visit Charlie ever made to a perpetual adoration chapel was with his godparents after Mass when we were visiting them. It was very special to see them interacting in this way, talking to him softly about the presence of Jesus. He was also quite taken with the stained glass windows, which both interested him and reminded us of their beauty. Seeing the world through the eyes of a child can be so powerful for your own faith life, and we could see how much joy he brought to his godparents during this moment.

Prayer Corner

Consider adding a picture frame or card celebrating the dates of each family member's baptism. You might also display your baptismal candles that frequently tend to gather dust in the back of closets. While preparing for the baptism of a new member of the family, display an image of the baptism of Christ. This image is a beautiful way to direct your thoughts toward Jesus during prayer time as you prepare your child to receive the sacrament.

A Wealth of Prayers

In the previous chapter, we explored traditional prayers that are great to use during your daily prayer routines. Here, we'll look at some prayers that you use only once or for special occasions. Some could be used during family prayer, while others are for your personal prayer as you pray for your child(ren).

Blessing for the Child in Utero

Did you know your child can be blessed in your womb? It is beautiful to bless your child early on in a pregnancy because it can help you to recognize the "real-ness" of your child. Ask your priest before or after Mass if he can bless your child in utero; priests are usually thrilled to do so! (If the pregnancy is still a secret, we recommend stepping into an area out of view, as he will probably make the sign of the cross in the air over your womb). Some priests will even perform a quick blessing when administering Communion, as they would for any other young child, which is a beautiful way of holding your child dear while receiving the Eucharist. There is also an official rite for blessing a child in the womb, recently approved by the Vatican. This is a lengthier blessing, which is more structured with specific blessings and responses. If your priest does not have the text already, it is available online or for order through the United States Conference of Catholic Bishops (USCCB).

Blessing for Mothers

The Churching of Women is a blessing that dates back to the early Christian church and has fallen out of practice, but is still very much available for use. Even if your priest is unaware of this blessing, he should be able to find its text and directions with ease. This blessing bestows grace upon the mother to help her to raise her child in the faith. This blessing is meant for the mother, but also greatly benefits her child.

> *Michele writes:*
>
> *When my husband first told me about the practice of the* **Churching of Women** *I was a bit skeptical. Wasn't it something old-fashioned? It wasn't at all! I felt so blessed and special when I received this blessing from my priest and it was so nice to know that everyone celebrated my recovery from childbirth in this way. It's hard work giving birth to a little one and taking care of a newborn, and it's nice that the Church has a blessing to acknowledge all you've been through and to allow you to thank God for the gift of your little one.*

Household Blessings

It also used to be more common for pastors to perform a Blessing of the Home for the households in his parish. You can still invite your priest over to perform this ritual blessing if your home has not yet been blessed. It is a beautiful way to prepare for the arrival of a new family member. During this blessing, he will lead you in some prayers and sprinkle holy water throughout the rooms of the house. If your house has already been blessed, you can instead personally ask God's blessing to rain down upon your child's bed or crib. You can also sprinkle holy water on the bed during the blessing. Here is a simple prayer you can use for this purpose:

Lord you bless your followers in many ways.
Send forth this blessing, now we pray:
For our new child, bless this bed
Where (he/she) will lay (his/her) head
So that each night as (he/she) sleeps
You will (his/her) safety keep.
Amen.

Baptismal Prayer

In the days leading up to the baptism of your child, you can pray for him using any form of prayer you prefer. Here is one prayer of preparation for baptism you can pray daily:

Heavenly Father, protect this child,
Open (his/her) soul to receive the Holy Spirit.
Prepare (him/her) to receive you and your outpouring
  of grace,
In the beautiful sacrament of baptism.
We thank you and praise you for our own baptisms,
And ask that you aid us on the lifelong journey
  of parenthood
To help our child carry out (his/her) baptismal promises,
In order to spend eternal life with you.
Amen.

Activities

ACTIVITY 1: *SPIRITUALLY ENROLL YOUR CHILD*

Spiritual enrollment involves sending a small donation to a church or order of your choosing in exchange for the offering of prayers and Masses for someone. You are usually also gifted a card as a commemoration of this spiritual gift. This can be displayed somewhere in the home, such as in the prayer corner or in the child's room above his or her bed.

A large number of churches and organizations offer spiritual enrollment opportunities. To give you a better idea of what is entailed, let's look at an example. The National Shrine of the Immaculate Conception offers several options, including a one-year membership and a perpetual membership. When individuals are enrolled in one of these programs, they are remembered in a special Prayer Guild Novena of Masses offered the last nine days of each month, and are prayed for during the daily offering of the rosary.

To spiritually enroll your child, a simple Internet search reveals a plethora of options. Alternatively, you can call a monastery or church of your choosing to see if it offers any spiritual enrollment programs. Typically, larger organizations offer them, but if you are interested in a particular church or faith-based organization, it never hurts to ask them if they have a spiritual enrollment option.

ACTIVITY 2: *MAKE A SPIRITUAL BOUQUET*

A spiritual bouquet is an offering of prayers and/or devotional acts for the sake of another person. Offering a spiritual bouquet for a new child is a beautiful way to prepare for and celebrate a little one's baptism. All members of the family can participate as they are able to in this offering. Here is a list of some prayers and devotional acts you could include in your spiritual bouquet:

- Pray common prayers such as the Our Father, Hail Mary, Glory Be, etc.

- Recite the rosary, a decade of the rosary, or some other devotional prayer, such the Chaplet of Divine Mercy

- Offer a **novena**. Novenas are collections of prayers to God that can also be said through the intercession of a specific saint over a period of several days (generally nine). As emphasized earlier, the original novena was said to be in upper room as the disciples awaited the Advocate (Holy Spirit) after Jesus ascended into heaven; liturgically there are nine days between Ascension and Pentecost. Each novena is unique in the prayers it offers and can vary in duration. Some novenas may be found in Catholic prayer books. They can also be found at Catholic bookstores, online, and are sometimes provided in your church. Try searching for a novena to the Holy Spirit or to a saint to whom you are attracted. A saint who is a parent, such as Saint Joseph or Saint Monica, would be an especially fitting choice. A novena to the Holy Spirit might be particularly appropriate as you prepare for your child's baptism.

- Attend a daily Mass or pay a small donation to offer a Mass for your child.
- Light candles in the church as an offering, or in the home as you whisper a prayer.
- Visit shrines or altars in order to offer up prayers for the child.
- Perform good deeds and offer your gifts in community service.
- Make charitable donations such as one to your church, an order you are dedicated to, a shrine dedicated to a saint she is named after, etc.

When you have completed your spiritual bouquet, it is common to create some sort of keepsake to commemorate these prayers, such as a card or certificate. This is then gifted to the recipient. In this case, the recipient is your young child, so consider making something that can be saved in his or her baby book. It can also grace your prayer corner for a short while, either while you are completing the spiritual bouquet, or once it has been completed.

Michele writes:

For Therese's baptism, we gave her the gift of a spiritual bouquet. We asked our family and friends to send us letters and e-mails telling us what special prayers they were offering for her in the days leading up to her baptism. Then, we put all the letters and e-mails in a book for her to read when she gets older. Hopefully, it will help her to know how loved she was (and is!) as a member of the Church.

This is a wonderful activity for young children to participate in while a younger sibling is prepared for baptism. Use
the "Prayer in the Home" chapter as a guide for incorporating your child into the prayers at an age appropriate level. An
older child can participate further by helping decorate the
commemorative card gifted to the infant.

ACTIVITY 3: *BAPTISM ROLE PLAY*

Although your infant will not be able to understand what is happening to her when she is baptized, you will be able to talk to her about it when she is older. Likewise, older siblings will not remember their own baptisms and may benefit from a refresher course before the baptism of a baby brother or sister. Some simple role playing can be a fun and easy way for little ones to learn about baptism...and to remember what they learned!

You will need:
- a baby doll (preferably one that is plastic or at least has a plastic head)
- a large bowl (the more beautiful the better!)
- a small cup or sea shell
- water
- a towel

1. Fill up the large bowl with water. Set it on a large towel (in case of spills). Invite your child to help in these preparations.

2. Dress the baby doll in white clothes (if you have them) or wrap the doll in a white towel or cloth.

3. Tell your child that you are going to learn about baptism. Tell him or her that baptism is the sacrament that welcomes us into the Church. Then continue to tell the child about his or her own baptism, and maybe look at some pictures of family baptisms together.

4. Now tell your little one that you are going to learn the words of the baptismal rite together, and that these are the words that the priest or deacon will use to baptize someone (if there is a baptism coming up soon in your family, make the connection to the upcoming event!).

5. Take the baby doll, and say, "Do you see this doll? We are going to pretend that this doll is a baby who is getting baptized. Do you see how she is wearing white? She is wearing white to show that she is going to be washed clean of original sin through her baptism. I'm going to pour some water over her head—like the priest would do—and say the words that he says when he baptizes a baby or a grown-up."

6. Now, holding the baby doll over the bowl of water, pour water over the doll's head (using the cup or shell) while saying, "I baptize you in the name of the Father," pour more water, "...and of the Son," pour more water, "..and of the Holy Spirit. Amen!" Invite your child to act this out, too. Ask your little one if he or she has any questions. This activity can be utilized with toddlers, preschoolers, or even big kids.

For the Record

FIRST YEAR

My child's baptism occurred on _____.

This is the feast day of Saint _____

_____ .

It was performed by _____

at _____

Name _____

Godparents are _____

_____

_____

We chose them to be godparents because _____

_____

_____

_____

Some other attendees at this event were _____

_____

_____

_____

_____

We prepared for the baptism by _____

_____

_____

_____

During the baptism, you wore _____

_____

_____

Description of the baptism: _____

_____

_____

_____

_____

_____

_____

_____

We celebrated your baptism by _____

_____

_____

_____

_____

_____

Some gifts you received in celebration of your baptism in-

clude _____

_____

_____

_____

_____

_____

_____

_____

_____

_____

Chapter 4

THE MASS WITH LITTLE ONES

Michele shares:

Before having Therese, I had all sorts of wonderful ideas about what bringing her to Mass would be like. She would sit quietly for most of the time (of course), preferably flipping quietly through religious picture books with me while gazing adoringly at the altar from time to time. I knew that many little ones that I saw at Mass didn't behave this way, and I knew that there was a small chance that the baby I carried inside me for those nine long months might behave like those other children at Mass...but surely she would be the exception. Surely having two parents with a combined ten years of theology studies would equal one perfectly behaved child at Mass.

Then, Therese entered the world. She was a normal baby. She slept at Mass (on rare blissful occasions), and she would sometimes sit or lay peacefully in the arms of her parents. But she also cried at Mass. She fussed and babbled at Mass (a lot). She got ravenously hungry during Mass and had to be taken out and nursed. She had to be paced with in the back of the church, and we even had to take her to the cry room on occasion. Worst of all, she would sometimes let loose an explosive poop right at the beginning of the eucharistic prayer, causing me to miss most (if not all) of the rest of the Mass as I toted her off to the ladies' room to attend to the toxic waste disposal.

But surely, surely, I thought...toddlerhood would be better. We had been taking her to daily and Sunday Mass since she was about a week old, and surely that would pay off as she approached her first birthday.

Therese is a normal toddler. She rests in my lap and flips through religious books with me. She will point to "Jeez!" (Jesus) and "Mare!" (Mary). She will sweetly fold her hands and ask to "pray" at some points during and after Mass. She will also have screaming fits in the middle of Mass, throw tantrums when we won't let her run up the aisle, and she briefly developed a pathological fear of returning to the pew (after needing to step out during said tantrum). She pretends that the kneeler is a "car" and is very upset when she is not allowed to ride her "car" during the entire Mass. She bangs books down on the pew, and throws her milk down, dousing the pew and surrounding areas with it. Worst of all, she's caused even more trips to the cry room and the back of the church and drained more patience out of her parents than we ever thought possible.

There have most certainly been days when I've wondered, "Well, couldn't we just sit in the cry room and let her play during Mass? Couldn't we even just leave her home sometimes with a babysitter?" And yet it seems that none of those options would solve the problem of teaching her how to behave at Mass.

It is tempting, I'll admit, to altogether give up until our girl reaches the age of reason. However, were we to do that, we would miss a precious and beautiful window of time in her faith life. True, those under the age of seven have not yet attained the use of their reason. True, those under the age of three have not really yet attained the full use of language. Yet, taking these little ones to Mass can reap many benefits.

Let the Little Ones Come to Me

As Catholic parents, we have a unique opportunity to truly immerse our little ones in the faith life. Yes, it is important that they learn to be quiet at Mass. But it is even more important that they become immersed in the life of the Church. Just as, from the youngest of ages, we do all we can to incorporate our babies and toddlers into our family life, we must do likewise when it comes to immersing them in the family of the Church.

Usually a child is prepared for his or her first Communion when the age of reason has been reached and is usually prepared through religious education classes of some sort. However, preparation should start outside of the classroom long before this age is reached. The absolute best way to teach a little one about the Eucharist is to start from the very beginning. The best way to start teaching a child about the Eucharist is when he or she is still within the mother's womb (or, in the case of an adoptive child, praying for him or her prior to birth or his or her entrance into your family). Remember that even mothers who do not physically carry their children may still spiritually carry them with the beautiful prayer that only a mother can offer. The role of an adoptive mother is just as important as a physical mother when it comes to praying for and nurturing the spiritual life of your little one before birth!

Michele shares:

Some of my most precious memories of my pregnancy with Therese were in the moments after I would receive the Eucharist at Mass. I would have Jesus inside of me, and I would have Therese inside of me. Though Therese wasn't receiving the Eucharist, I knew from my eucharistic theology that, when we receive Jesus in the Eucharist, we become like walking tabernacles—a place where our Lord dwells. This meant that, although my little girl was too small to receive Jesus in the Eucharist, she was not too small to rest beside him within me. She was not too small or too young to be loved by him in this special way. And so, during this time, I would whisper a prayer. I would first tell my little Therese (who I knew could hear my voice even if she couldn't understand my words) that Jesus was close to her because he was resting inside of Mommy. Then I would pray for her—I would pray that she would be born safely and led to the waters of baptism. I prayed for her vocation. I prayed that she would grow to love Jesus more and more each day. I held her close to my mother's heart for those long nine months—but the most precious moments were when I held her close to Jesus in the Eucharist, resting inside of me. I knew then that I was laying the foundations for her to know the love of God.

When she was born and soon after she was baptized, I continued praying for the baby who was now in my arms. After she was baptized, I knew that she had been gifted with special grace—grace that made her more open to God in her life. I knew that my responsibility was now far greater because she had become an adopted child of God through the waters of baptism. My job was no longer just to lead her to God, but rather to lead her to grow in her relationship with God. Our prayers post-Communion became whispered requests that she might receive spiritual Communion—a very close union with Jesus for those who cannot receive the Eucharist for whatever reason—until that day when she received Jesus in the Eucharist for the first time.

For years I worked with individuals with disabilities, some with very severe disabilities. If there is one thing that I learned from my time with them it is this—one's mental capacity does not determine one's ability to develop a relationship with Jesus in the Eucharist. Rather, openness to grace and time spent with Jesus in the Eucharist—these are what lead to a relationship of love. From this experience, I knew that the same was true for my little newborn with her own limited mental capabilities. I knew that she did not need a well-developed reason to know the truth of Jesus' presence in the Eucharist. All she needed was to experience it. She needed to be taken to adoration and Mass (even daily Mass, when possible). She needed time to just be with Jesus.

Amy shares:

Like Michele, I absolutely love receiving Communion while pregnant. As I walk back from the Communion line, I ask God to strengthen my child, just as he strengthens me with the Eucharist. In this way, I am praying for my child's spiritual communion with God. My child cannot experience the same physical communion we as adults can, but I am always *reminded at this time to pray for a spiritual nourishment of his young faith. Now that Charlie is born, I cuddle him close after Communion (unless my husband is holding him, then it's his job!). I love the feeling I get walking back from the Communion line, praying that Christ strengthens me and also strengthens my little guy. I also think of God the Father's love for me and how he loves me even more than I could ever love my children. It's a great reminder, and I am in awe of it, especially considering how much love I feel in those moments. I think to myself, wow, how wonderful is God that he could love this much. God loves me more than I can ever think possible, and I realize that I am called to love my child even beyond my own ability to do so. Then I ask God to continually increase my love for my children.*

I also like to think about the fact that I am called to dedicate my life first and foremost to Christ in order to serve that little bundle in my arms. I spend a lot of the Mass focusing my energy on taking care of Charlie, but during that short walk back from Communion, I am able to focus my thoughts entirely on my vocation and my God. My parish has a beautiful stained glass window above the organ; I always meditate upon it while walking back to the pew. This very short window of uninterrupted prayer (sometimes only about fifteen seconds) is one of the most blissful moments of Mass for me.

We aren't suggesting here that, if you follow these suggestions, you will have a toddler who naturally lays prostrate at the mere sight of a tabernacle or monstrance. Hardly! That's where your role as a parent comes in—teaching your little one to genuflect, etc. This is important, because this is one way we show our love for Jesus in the Eucharist, and can be likened to the way you might teach your little one to kiss Grandma. It is vital that they learn to show respect and love for all, especially our Lord in the Eucharist.

But your time in adoration and at Mass with your little one is about more than just teaching her to say "Jesus!" whenever she sees the tabernacle (although it's pretty cute once they learn to say that!). It's less about her end and more about God's purpose for her life. As any parent of a newborn knows, a young child does not always know how to ask for what he needs. A baby may cry, but it's up to a parent to determine if a diaper needs to be changed or a belly fed. Our jobs as parents are to be sure that they are where they need to be to have their needs met—on the changing table, pulled close to the mother to nurse, rocked in a swing to sleep. Similarly, we are called to bring them to Jesus in the Eucharist—through adoration, at Mass, or even through a short visit to the tabernacle—because they need to be with him. They need to be loved in the special way that only Jesus can love them. They need to have the opportunity to be with him and let him work on their hearts—no matter how small they may be!

This is not to say that this is always feasible. There are days—and sometimes many days in a row—when it simply isn't feasible to bring your little one to church for any number of reasons. God knows a parent's heart and knows those reasons well. However, when it is possible to bring your little one to be with Jesus—especially at Mass—know that what you are doing is of utmost importance. By that simple act, you are beginning what will hopefully lead to a lifelong relationship of love with Jesus in the Eucharist.

Sensory Experiences

We are very fortunate as Christian parents to be raising infants and toddlers in the Catholic Church. The Catholic Church is sacramental in two ways: (1) through the sacraments we can tangibly experience the holiness of God, and (2) creation reflects God and tells us of our Lord's majestic glory. As Catholics, God calls us to sanctify the world and not to run from it. God calls us to take that which is ordinary, offer it up in prayer, and allow it to be made into something holy. For example, Catholic churches are traditionally constructed with a definite appeal to the senses. This is true to some degree, no matter how long ago or recently a Church was constructed. Beautiful icons, stained glass windows, candles, paintings of saints, statuaries, shining gold tabernacles, chalices and patens made of precious medals, the scent of incense, the cool trickling of holy water in the baptismal font—all experiences to be had in Catholic churches across the globe. All these features appeal to the senses—the colors, textures, sounds, smells, and even taste.

Fortunately, infants and toddlers are at an age where the primary way that they learn is through the senses. Yes, these little ones will sometimes comprehend what you are trying to tell them with words, but the way that they learn best is through experiences. The Internet and books are abuzz these days with ideas for sensory experiences for your young child— everything from sensory bins to messy play. Who knew that going to Mass could be the ultimate sensory experience?

The Mass, and a Catholic church in general, are excellent places for sensory learning. Focusing on sensory learning is an ideal way to engage even the smallest of children in the Mass. The next time you find yourself in your parish, take a few moments to see the church through the eyes of your child.

Is anything shiny? Shimmery? What sounds do you hear? What scents do you smell? What do you find soothing? What is beautiful? What is strikingly different from the things you see at home? These sensory elements can serve as a springboard for catechizing your little one during Mass.

For example, there are often beautiful **statues** or **paintings** scattered throughout each church (some churches may only have a few while others may be replete with them!). When your little one reaches his or her inevitable point of restlessness and you find yourself pacing in the back of the church, try to find one of these beautiful images.

Michele shares:

When Therese was small, we used to go to Mass at a church with a beautiful, very colorful icon of the Holy Family in the very back. So, as I paced with our girl, I would periodically stop at the icon and point it out to her, using simple words to talk about it. "Look! Do you see this beautiful picture of the Holy Family? Is that Jesus? And Mary? And Saint Joseph? Look! Jesus is a tiny baby, just like you!"

Amy shares:

As Charlie started walking, all he wanted to do was be in-dependent and run around the church—which also meant that he was finding things he shouldn't get into, and we were constantly grabbing him and attempting to redirect him so he wouldn't wander away. To avoid this, we tried holding him and directing his attention to things he finds interesting. After learning the word "Jesus," I started walking around the back of the church and in the side chapel, pointing to various images of Christ and repeating the word "Jesus." He is also very interested in lights and likes to point to the lights while making the sign language sign for "light." In an attempt to direct this interest back to the Mass in some form, I whisper, "Yes, that is a light! Do you see these lights?" and point to candles on the tabernacle.

Because Mass is filled with activity, movement, and plenty of visual aides, it's easy to apply this mode of learning to the Mass itself. This learning can even be accomplished in such a way that it teaches your little one some of the basic vocabulary of the Mass. For example, when the reader stands up to read the first reading, you can say, "Look! Do you see the **lector**? The lector is doing the reading!" The **priest** is our go-to man in moments of fussiness (this is all the more helped by the fact that we have been blessed with some wonderful priests in the life of our little girl). At any given point, it can help your little one to refocus by playing a simple game of, "Where's the priest?" Once you find the priest, there may be something else to discuss together. "Look! There's the priest. He's holding Jesus in the Eucharist!"

The **crucifix** at the front of each church can also be a basic focal point for your little one. Each time you enter your church, you can point out the crucifix to him or her and say, "Look! Do you see the Jesus there on the cross?" Even more poignant is locating the tabernacle, because then you can say, "Look! Do you see the **tabernacle**? Jesus is there," opening up the door to teach your littlest one about the Eucharist.

Even before your child can fully understand what it means for Jesus to be truly present in the Eucharist, you can still give them simple reminders by pointing to the host and saying, "Look! That's Jesus in the **Eucharist**. Isn't that so special? He is right here with us, in this special way, because he loves us!" In future years, when your little one receives the Eucharist for the first time, it will be a sensory-filled experience (as all the sacraments are, really). But right now, the Eucharist appeals to her sense of sight—gazing at Christ present in this hidden way, and learning to rest her eyes on him in the midst of this restless world. Your child is never too young to learn this.

Cry Rooms, Nurseries, and Children's Liturgies

Once you have your first child, you have a myriad of decisions to make, and that doesn't stop when you walk through the church doors. When should you take your child to the cry room? Should you stay in the cry room from the beginning of Mass to the very end? What do you do when there isn't a cry room? Should you just leave your child in the church's nursery? Should you send your child to the children's liturgy? Unfortunately there are no single right answers for these questions. You may feel pulled in different directions regarding these issues, especially if some individuals are outspoken in their opinions on these matters. The best answer to these questions is the answer that works best for your family and your child in each situation. Let's look at some of these possibilities in greater detail.

The cry room: Not all churches have them, and not all of them are the same. There might be one young mother in this room soothing her crying infant, or it might be filled to the brim with entire families who bring their children of all ages so that their preschooler can play with his car toys as loudly as he chooses for the whole Mass, racing up and down the aisles. The best way to approach the cry room is to use it only when necessary. Ultimately, you must decide when it is and is not necessary, and this is the part that varies from family to family. However, we would like to encourage you to respect others at all times when using a cry room. Even though it is meant to accommodate our less-than-quiet children, this should not encourage noise for the sake of noise.

Keep in mind that while in the cry room, you are still at Mass. Make your best attempt to participate in the Mass, and to allow others to do the same. For example, if your child is throwing an all-out screaming tantrum (it happens!), carefully consider your options. Is the cry room filled with others making a more-than-minimal amount of noise? If so, you might consider relocating to the narthex (the entrance or lobby of the church) until your child is calmer. Most churches pipe their sound systems into this area as well. On the other hand, if the cry room is empty, make full use of it. Remember that usually there are adults in the cry room as well, and they—like you—would like to be able to pay some sort of attention to the Mass. This means that your child should still be taught to be quiet, if possible. We must work to teach them to behave properly at Mass. The cry room is intended for our young ones who are having trouble remaining quiet, but we ought to be mindful of the notion that our young ones might find it rewarding to go there for playtime; when possible seize opportunities to nurture prayer even in the cry room by attempting to teach silence, reverence, nurture, etc.

Amy shares:

When we were visiting another parish, I tried to use the cry room (Charlie was being fussy). I was horrified. Parents were participating in the Mass, but many of them were completely ignoring their children. The adults didn't seem to care what their children were doing, how loud they were screaming, or how distracting they were being, as long as they didn't leave the room. I came in to soothe my baby so he wouldn't bother others, but instead, we could barely hear the Mass and the noise was bothering him more. In this case, we found the cry room did not meet the prayer needs of either ourselves or those of our child. I ended up walking back and forth with him in the narthex in front of the glass doors, where I could still see and hear what was going on in Mass. Once he calmed down, I was able to move back inside, behind the last pew, where I could sway and soothe Charlie and still participate in Mass.

Our parish does not have a cry room. As first-time parents, we were really worried about being a huge bother to others. But we soon realized that some crying was expected by the parish since they knew there was no cry room. In addition, we started to get a little creative. The parish has a gathering area, or narthex, that we often use for sudden all-out screaming fits, or when it is too difficult to keep our son settled. We attend a historic parish and sit on the side of the church near a small chapel. When Charlie gets overly fussy, we simply step into the side chapel, where we as parents can still usually see the priest, but Charlie isn't being quite as distracting to others. Not only is he farther away from them physically, the acoustics of the side chapel *are such that he is not as noticeable to others in the parish (the church tends to echo). There is a back exit out of the chapel where we can easily head to the rear of the church if necessary. There is a large space behind the last pew where I spend quite a bit of time walking around with him, also with quick access to the narthex, should the decibel level increase suddenly.*

The nursery provides a different option than a cry room—a place where you can drop your child off at the beginning of Mass and pick him up after it is over. It's sort of like a babysitter you bring to church with you. Again, like the cry room, we encourage you to only make use of this option when absolutely necessary. Unfortunately, it may be necessary at times, especially with a high-needs child or during a particularly rough phase of temper tantrums. There is no sin in this option. Keep in mind that the best way to teach your child about the Mass is to bring him to the Mass. In fact, it is often easier for children to behave well at Mass if they are taught to do so from an earlier age. If you wait until they are older to bring them to Mass, they may find the time spent at church to be boring in comparison to that fun room with toys they used to be able to visit.

Some parishes provide children's liturgy programs for preschoolers and young children (who have not yet made their first Communion). In programs like this, the children usually start off Mass with their family, are sent away before the Liturgy of the Word with a blessing, and return before the Liturgy of the Eucharist (though this varies from program to program). Is this program a good fit for the preschooler in your family? Well, that depends. We would encourage you to ask questions about how the program is run and see if you can attend it once yourself to see just what is included. Only then can you make a fully informed decision. If you feel comfortable with the level of catechesis, interaction, and reverence provided by the program, you may wish to send your child to the children's liturgy. If, however, you feel your preschooler is thriving at Mass with you, there really is no reason to send her away for part of it. Another option to consider is allowing your child to go to the children's liturgy program a certain number of times a month. At some parishes, they may only offer this type of program once or twice a month anyway, making this a non-issue. As your children grow older, it would be best to "wean" them off of the program by sending them less and less frequently, instead of sending them out of Mass every week until they hit a certain age, and then abruptly discontinuing their participation. Again, as with the nursery, they will at some point need to attend the entire Mass every week with you as a family. The less regularly they attend a full Mass, the more difficult the transition will be. You may also opt out of using the children's Liturgy of the Word entirely. There is much to be said for training little ones to be present in the Mass itself, for you can help them understand what is happening in the readings if you talk about them with your child before or after Mass.

What About the Parents?

We've been talking a lot about how you as a family will encounter the Mass, but what about you as individuals? As adults? The need to receive Christ into your being (heart, body, and soul), catechetical instruction, and a participation with full heart and voice in the Mass do not simply disappear with the arrival of your child. How, then, are you to juggle everything so that Mass is still the foundation of your faith life?

There are a number of ways to approach this issue, and no one way is right for everyone. Participating well in the Mass depends on both you and your child's needs and personality—there are many different ways to take part. For example, your child will surely reach an age at which her single biggest desire for the entire hour is to confiscate the missalette and/or hymnal from you. Depending on how much you usually rely on these books, this can be quite a disruption. Your ability to participate in singing may be hampered, and your attention may not be as focused during the readings. When something is going on that consistently disrupts a normal part of your Mass routine, it's time to get creative. Ask yourself two questions: (1) What is the purpose of this part of Mass? and (2) How can I achieve that same goal in a slightly different way? During hymns you do not know, your spouse may be able to commandeer the hymnal, you may be able to hum along instead if you know the tune, or you may simply pray by listening to the words of the hymn. If you rely on the printed daily readings to help you focus during the Liturgy of the Word, take the time to read the Scripture passages before going to Mass. These are just a few examples, but the concept can be applied throughout the Mass. Think creatively about adaptations you may need to make so that you can participate in Mass in the fullest manner possible. Remember, too, that the most important prayer that God is calling you to offer now is the prayer of loving care for your child...even if that means you don't always remember the message given in the homily.

With children running around your feet and spitting up

down your back (we've all been there), it's so easy to feel like you aren't "getting anything out of it." Why even go to Mass when you can hardly follow what's going on? As Michele pointed out earlier, there will be those times you yearn to simply hire a weekly Sunday babysitter so you can at least know what is taking place at Mass. Rather than resorting to childcare, see what other options you have. It's not wrong to take an occasional break for mental health—so decide a good way to work it out for your family. Maybe you can find that quiet you seek by attending adoration or a daily Mass alone once a week so that your attention can remain undivided. Take turns being the main care provider during Sunday Masses. If you live by relatives or attend the same parish as close friends, see if they can sometimes sit with you. They'll love to hold your little ones when Mommy and Daddy aren't needed, and this may relieve some stress for the two of you.

The summit of the Mass is the Liturgy of the Eucharist. The host and wine are transformed into the Body and Blood, soul and divinity of Jesus Christ. Logistically speaking, you need to consider how you will receive the Eucharist. If your child is old enough to walk well and up to speed, you may have him walk in line in front of you (or to the side, if this is not disruptive to another line). Obviously you should not have him follow you and assume all is going well. Your preschooler, though capable of many things, also still possesses much curiosity, and she should be within your line of vision and arm's reach at all times. If your child is not old enough to walk appropriately in the Communion line, you will need to carry her. What happens as you reach the extraordinary minister or priest? To receive Communion in the hand—the most common form of reception in the United States—one must have two hands free. Your dominant hand is placed under your nondominant hand. (Let's assume you are right-handed—this means the Eucharist is placed into your left hand, which acts as a throne for Christ. You then pick up the host with your right hand, place it in your mouth, and consume it immediately.) If one or both hands are tied up holding a child, you will not be able to correctly receive in the hand. In this case, you may want to make use of a baby sling or carrier of some sort to free up your hands during this time. Alternatively, there is also the option of receiving on the tongue.

If you need to receive on the tongue, don't be nervous. Simply open your mouth and be sure to extend your tongue well enough for the host to fit. It's as easy as that. If you are worried or unsure about this practice, try sitting in an area where the priest distributes Communion until you gain confidence. They administer Communion far more frequently than extraordinary ministers do, and even if it is not common practice at your parish, priests are well-trained in administering Communion on the tongue. It is not our goal to push you to receive in one manner or another—both reception in the hands and on the tongue are considered acceptable at English Masses. We merely point out these scenarios as options to help you receive the Eucharist correctly, with reverence and love.

Prayer Corner

Something simple you may wish to include in your prayer corner would be a picture of your church or pastor. When your family gathers together to pray before bedtime, you can point to the picture and ask your child to join you in praying for your church or priest by name.

A Wealth of Prayers

The entire Mass is a prayer, but before, within, and after the Mass there are opportunities for quiet, private prayer. During these times, we encourage you to pray for your children or quietly whisper the words of your prayers into their ears so that they can take part. These prayer times may take many forms. You may simply speak the words on your heart, pray a more traditional prayer like the Our Father, or make use of some of the following prayers:

Prayer Before Mass

> *Dear Lord,*
> *Christ invited the little ones to go to him*
> *Here we bring* (insert name or names of your children)
> *   to witness the mystery of the sacrament*
> *Bless them to receive your grace and to know your love*
> *Help them to encounter you in their small ways.*
> *Amen.*

Prayer After Receiving Communion

> *Oh my God,*
> *Your Son lovingly gave us this gift of his Body and Blood.*
> *Strengthen me in my vocation as a parent through the*
> *   holy Eucharist.*
> *Grant me the grace to give fully of myself each day,*
> *   in imitation of Jesus.*
> *I ask you to bestow these same graces upon*
> *   (name of child)*
> *That (s)he may grow in holiness,*
> *Becoming a child of faith.*
> *Amen.*

Prayer for a Child to Receive Spiritual Communion

> *Dear Jesus, thank you for this gift of the Eucharist.*
> *Please grant* (child's name) *the grace of spiritual*
>   *Communion*
> *that he/she may love you and long for you with all*
>   *his/her heart.*
> *We love you so much, dear Jesus! Amen.*

Prayer After Mass

> *Lord, we thank you for your gift of the Mass.*
> *Guide us and bless us as a family*
> *To always discern your will and follow your ways.*
> *Amen.*

Activities

ACTIVITY 1: *A MASS KIT*

Traditional toys can sometimes be a distraction at Mass, as there is an ordinary nature to them that detracts from the sacredness of Mass. However, little aides for helping a child stay focused and calm at Mass can be a wonderful thing.

When considering what "toys" your child should have in Mass, ask yourself, *"Can these things help my little one think about God and the Mass?"* There is a time and a place for non-religious toys, but consider the option for toys at Mass that do more than merely distract and entertain your little one. Could they assist you to help your little one pray? Even if your child is too young to pay attention during the entire Mass, having "toys" such as religious picture books, holy cards, plastic saint statues, or Catholic toys found at your local Catholic bookstore or online will give your little one something to hold and touch. This will also help your child to understand that Mass is a special place, the home of our Lord where we behave in a reverent way. Mass is a glimpse of heaven. Being at Mass is an opportunity to rest in God's love, away from the noisiness and concerns of daily life. Having special Mass "toys" like this will teach your child about the Mass as a "special place" without you having to say a word.

Here are some ideas for putting together your own go-to kit for Mass with your child:

1. Find a sturdy bag. Maybe you have one lying around the house, but you can also find one at a craft store. Or, you could simply use a diaper bag. If you want to dedicate the bag solely to this purpose, you may consider labeling it "Mass Bag" or "My Mass Kit." You can do this with a fabric marker (available at any craft store). You may even want to draw a picture of a chalice or host, etc.

2. Fill the bag with items that will help your young one to understand the life of Jesus. Here are some ideas:

- Felt is a lovely medium because it is cheap, versatile, and child-safe. Out of the felt, cut out some basic shapes (a chalice/golden cup, a paten/golden plate, a cross, etc.) that can be tucked in to your Mass kit and used as visual aides. Alternately, you can purchase stiff felt for a more durable material or you can even laminate construction paper shapes.

- Add books! Take a trip to your local Catholic bookstore or browse one online. There are many wonderful and affordable Catholic children's books available. There are also numerous inexpensive holy cards available for purchase (you can sometimes even find free holy cards at the back of your church). Use these simple picture books and holy cards to round out your Mass kit and personalize it for your child's interests. (For example, if your toddler has just learned to say "Mary," you may wish to put in a picture book about Mary and a few holy cards with her image.)

- You may wish to add in additional religious items suitable for children's prayerful play if you have them or are able to find them. Sometimes all you need to do is get a bit creative and use adult religious articles that are safe for a child's use—such as a small plastic statue of a favorite saint. Online handmade websites (such as Etsy.com) are excellent resources for good Catholic toys. Bring objects representing saints, priest or nun dolls/figurines, a child's rosary, or a small (and sturdy) crucifix. Be mindful that the smaller the child, the bigger the objects placed in the kit (an adult rosary is generally not appropriate for an infant).

You certainly don't need to bring all of these things to Mass at once—be prepared for the possibility that your child might pick up the bag and dump everything out. Only pack what is necessary to help your child focus. Consider rotating some objects in and out of the bag to keep things interesting. Once your Mass kit is complete, bring it along with you to Mass and offer it to your child if he or she grows restless, engaging her as necessary. Children can pray through their focused play and interactions with these religious objects.

ACTIVITY 2: *MY OWN MASS BOOK*

Infants love to gaze at pictures, and once toddlers begin learning words they develop a thirst for new vocabulary. Preschoolers are tackling the beginning steps of literacy and are eager to see the written word. Why not capitalize on each of these stages of development by teaching them the names of some important things found in your church? With tools as simple as a camera and a photo album (or scrapbook), you can provide your child with a **personalized Mass book**.

Begin by taking pictures of some of the important things found in your church, as well as some of your child's personal favorite sights. Some examples could include:

- **cross** and **crucifix**
- **altar**
- **ambo** (the podium where the readings and Gospel are read)
- **chalice** and **paten** (these are often found near the altar before Mass, and if you cannot find them you can ask your priest or sacristan if you can take a picture of them)
- **cruets** with water and wine (found in the back of the church before Mass to be taken up when the gifts are brought up at the offertory)
- **ciborium** with **hosts** (also found at the back of the church)
- **icons** or other pictures of saints

- **Stations of the Cross**
- **Tabernacle**
- **Statues**
- **Candles**

Once you have taken your pictures, put them in your photo album or scrapbook. Label them with their names (use the names above as a guide). Give the completed book to your child before or during Mass to help him or her to take a closer look at these important objects. Take time outside of the Mass as well to help children learn these words. Before or after Mass, spend a few moments walking around to match the items in the photographs with their location in the church. You can also include some of the prayers from the wealth of prayers given in each chapter to say or use at each Mass with your child.

For the Record

My child first attended Mass on _____

_____

_____

_____

_____

This is what he/she did during Mass _____

_____

_____

_____

_____

_____

My favorite story of my child at Mass is _____

_____

_____

_____

_____

_____

_____

My child's favorite part of the church building is _____

_____

_____

Some objects that helped my child focus during Mass includ-

ed_____

_____

Our parish name was _____

_____

_____

_____

The church looked like _____

_____

_____

_____

It had about _____ families

Our parish priests were _____

_____

_____

_____

We liked to sit _____

_____

_____

Other times we went to Mass besides Sundays included _____

_____

_____

_____

_____

A few church activities we attended outside of the Mass in-

cluded _____

_____

_____

_____

_____

_____

_____

_____

_____

Chapter 5

PRAYING THROUGH PLAY

Children play. It is simply what they do. Anything and every-thing can turn into a game, and often they pull the adults in their lives into the game as well. Their entire lives are filled with play. When considering how to form any person in their faith, it helps to consider the environment of the person. Youth ministers often do this, planning events around movie nights and other social gatherings. We also see this in other areas of the Church. Those wishing to form young families in the faith tend to work through children's faith formation programs, parish picnics, doughnut Sundays, etc. "Theology on Tap" caters to young adults by providing a relaxed atmosphere for them—one in which they can both learn about their faith and be surrounded by their peers.

Forming infants and toddlers in the faith is no different. We must consider what the world of an infant and toddler looks like when determining the best way to form them in the faith. Incidentally, the world of an infant or a toddler is one filled with play...so why not engage them there? The key is to immerse your child in the faith by surrounding him with things that remind him of his faith. Throughout the day, as he encounters the world around him, he will constantly encounter aspects of his Catholic life.

The Catholic Church has always sought to meet its members where they are and to teach them using tools and concepts they are capable of grasping. In the Middle Ages, when so much of the population could not read, beautiful paintings and stained glass windows populated churches. The idea was that those who could not read could still hear the stories of the Bible and the saints and see these stories depicted on the walls to help lift their hearts and minds upward. We must do the same with children by meeting them where they are while attempting to direct their thoughts upward to God. As parents, we can look to educational methods such as the Catechesis of the Good Shepherd (www.cgsusa.org) and the Montessori method as examples for this kind of approach.

Catechesis of the Good Shepherd

The Montessori method refers to a method of education and upbringing. You may have heard of Montessori schools, where this method transforms an ordinary classroom setting into a child-directed setting of learning and exploration. The environment is prepared carefully to appeal to the child's needs and senses. Interactive materials appropriate for the child's developmental stage are presented in an orderly and beautiful way to encourage the child to move throughout the space and interact with the various materials.

Catechesis of the Good Shepherd (CGS) is a catechetical (faith formation) program for children from preschool age on up. Its concepts are based on the Montessori method of education and can easily be adapted for younger ages as well. The CGS method beautifully illustrates what we are hoping to accomplish with our young ones by helping them assimilate faith in their infant, toddler, and preschool years.

CGS welcomes children into a prepared environment where they are able to learn about their faith. As is typical for Montessori environments, the furniture is small, the shelving is low, and everything is child-sized. This program uses objects that look like toys in order to teach the children about the faith. However, they use these objects in a more focused way than a child would ordinarily interact with their toys. The children learn to place the objects gently and to treat them with special care. Those teaching them speak with lowered voices and teach the children to do the same. They use these objects in a prayerful, quiet way, to help them draw closer to God.

All materials presented to the children are visual representations of some aspect of the faith in this program. These materials are also termed "works." One of the works is the altar work, which includes a child-sized altar, chalice, paten, altar cloth, etc. It is used to teach the child about the sacred vessels used during the Mass. Another series of works presents the parables. For example, in the parable of the Precious Pearl work, a small figurine is used, along with a small house and small baskets of pearls. These are used to quietly "act out" the story while a catechist reads it to the child. These are just a few examples of the many works and activities in the CGS program to illustrate how it meets the children where they are in order to help them learn about their faith in a relaxed and comfortable atmosphere. CGS refers to the child's "work," but it looks much like "play" to the adult! (This part of the book is based primarily on Michele's experience as an assistant within a CGS Level I atrium. For more information and to locate an atrium near you, visit www.cgsusa.org.)

Though CGS terms the child's "play" as "work," it is intended to fulfill the child's deep desires, not to be tiresome. For our purposes, it functions similar to "play." Maria Montessori taught time and again that for the very young child work is like play. In many cases it is the most fun play of all for them. CGS is designed for ages three to twelve, so it is perfect to start with your preschooler. This program can also serve as an inspiration when working with our infants and toddlers. We may even be able to share some of the lessons with them, with slight modifications.

While the play of toddlers and preschoolers is obvious, infants also "play" in their own way; through their basic interactions with you, they are engaging in a form of "play." It is certainly a much less structured play, where immersion is key. However, you can develop it into a more directed play as they grow and develop themselves. Even when that is not the case, though, this program—so distinctive from the widespread textbook-based faith formation programs—teaches us something valuable. The child can be engaged by means of the world that he or she is already familiar with: the world of play. (The catechetical program Godly Play works similarly, allowing a child to act out what he or she is learning, but using special objects and materials designed for that purpose. Godly play is focused more on "playing" than CGS is, but it is very similar in terms of the means of engaging the child. For more information on Godly Play, visit www.godlyplayfoundation.org.)

Preparing the Environment

In CGS, much like in any Montessori-style setting, the prepared environment (known as the "**atrium**") is key to the process of catechesis. The idea is that a prepared environment invites the child to learn and makes him or her want to engage in the process of catechesis. The catechists work hard to make the lighting just right (normally with as much natural lighting as possible) to display the materials as beautifully (on open, uncluttered shelving), and to keep the materials organized in a way that encourages the children to work with them. Similarly, we should view our own homes as the ultimate prepared environment. Obviously, we cannot turn our entire home into one large atrium, although that would be a lovely place to live, as anyone who has ever visited an atrium can attest. But we are called to make our homes into a place where the faith of our little ones can thrive.

In chapter 2, we explored the idea of making a prayer corner. The prayer corner is intended to be the heart of where your family's prayer will occur. But it needn't be

Although we cannot turn our entire home into one large atrium, we are called to make our homes into a place where the faith of our little ones can thrive.

the only place. This one small corner of the house now serves as inspiration for many other places within the house, both for prayer and for prayerful play. One of the things advocated in Montessori-prepared environments is hanging pictures at a level that the child can see them and to keep materials stored low, within easy reach for the child. This idea can be adapted to work well in your own home. If you don't want to hang a lot of low items on your walls, make good use of shelving space and child-sized tables instead. You may find some areas in the home where you can hang items low on the walls—such as in a play space or bedroom.

Michele shares:

I was initially uncomfortable with the idea of hanging pictures low on my walls, as you may be, too. (And, to be entirely honest, I know that my husband wouldn't be thrilled with that particular mode of decorating since he likes to look at the pictures on our walls, too!) One small way that I prepare the environment for growing in faith in our home is to have religious images on shelves at toddler-eye level. I do have a low shelf and mirror hanging in my daughter's room, where she stands and sits to get dressed (with Mommy's help, of course!). On that little shelf, we now keep a holy card of her patron saint and the little crucifix I kept with me when I was in labor with her. Both of these serve as reminders for both of us of the infinite love that God has for us. The picture of her patron saint opens the door to talking to her, in simple language, about her patron saint. When I remember to, I tell her, "Look! Do you see the picture of Saint Therese? She's your patron saint. That means that she's your good friend in heaven, and she's always praying for you. Saint Therese, pray for us!" It's such a small thing, and I honestly forget most times, but I remember to talk to her about her patron saint more than I would if it weren't for that image!

This principle can carry over to toy areas, too, of course. In one area where Therese's learning toys are kept, I put a small icon of Mary and baby Jesus. (She loves pictures of baby Jesus!) It's a small reminder to both of us that all of our play and learning is given to God, as a gift of love. It's also a reminder to me to stay calm and patient with her in the midst of our time together. (As all parents of infants and toddlers know, there are some less-than-rosy moments with these little people!)

The next part of your environment that you have to pre-pare is yourself. You and your attitude are an important part of your child's environment. Much of what your child knows about the love of God will be learned through how you treat him or her. If you treat your child as an annoyance, frequently getting impatient and frustrated, then God's love for your child will be less poignantly felt. All of us parents, to be honest, are guilty of impatience at one time or another, and often it is because our own wells have run dry. As a parent, be sure to take time to rest, rejuvenate, and pray. You'll be a much better parent for it. Your interaction with your little one is an ongoing form of teaching that continues throughout every part of your child's day.

Take time to purposefully slow down your day. If you are a working parent who needs to drop your child off at daycare or with a babysitter, let your good-bye be as tender as pos-sible. As any working parent knows, leaving children in the care of another—even a relative—can be gut-wrenching for everyone involved. Many parents today are in a situation where this is unavoidable, and yet it can be a moment to show love to your little one in a unique way. Before saying good-bye to your child (no matter how old or young), take a moment to give him a small blessing. You can use words, or simply trace the sign of the cross on your little one's forehead when kiss-ing him good-bye. Throughout the day, as you think of your child, offer up a prayer for him. If it is particularly difficult for you to be apart from your child on a given day, why not offer up your sadness for him, asking Jesus to unite it to his own loving sacrifice on the cross?

Offering up the sufferings and sacrifices we endure as par-ents is the most beautiful way we can pray for our children. When you pick your little one up at the end of the day, shower him with love and affection. It is easy to just get right back in to the swing of the busyness of life, so take a moment to re-center yourself and remember that your children constantly learn from your actions. Say a prayer aloud as you buckle your littlest ones into car seats, thanking God for a good day and for the gift of your reunion. Keep little note cards with these prayers written on them and keep them in your wallet, around your house and your car, or simply make up prayers spontaneously. Taking moments like this throughout the day to pray constantly reminds us to find our strength from God, allows us a moment to calm ourselves down to be able to interact lovingly with our children, and teaches them that any time is a good time to talk to God.

If you are a stay-at-home parent, your main challenge is to maintain a sense of calm and patience, even in the midst of some very challenging moments. As you may have already experienced, your child's mood often reflects your own. In moments of particular frustration, it is helpful to slow down, lower your voice, and maybe say a quick prayer for the grace to be patient. As a stay-at-home parent, you have the unique opportunity to imbue your child's day with reminders of God's love for him. For example, you can say grace before all meals and snacks. When going for a walk together, point out the beauty of creation and say a simple prayer of thanks to God for that beauty. Try going to Mass together on a weekday, or making a brief visit to an adoration chapel together during the day. These may seem like small things, but they all work together to create an environment in which your little one may learn to recall God and his loving goodness through the day. You, too, can offer up difficult moments for your child, turning an otherwise frustrating situation into beautiful prayers of love.

Michele shares:

I've experienced both working and staying home with my daughter (as well as bringing my daughter to work) and I can honestly say that there are sufferings and sacrifices that a parent has to make regardless of the situation. It is easy on difficult days of working either at home or out of the home to become too focused on the sacrifices you are making and the sufferings you have to endure. I am very guilty of this. In those moments, it helps for me to offer up those difficulties for my daughter and to pray for the grace to keep going. We all know how easy it is to be loving toward our children when they are well-behaved and well-rested. However, it is in these moments—in the midst of an infant's crying fit or a toddler's tantrum—that we are most called to show God's love. Every parent has a different way of responding to these moments, since every child is different, but no matter how you respond you can pray that your response may be a loving one.

Sometimes, when Therese is having a tantrum I know she needs a time-out. As much as I'm tempted to, that's not the moment to shove her in her crib and slam her door, yelling as I go. (Oh, it is so tempting, though!) Far more helpful to her is when I am able to respond with (outward) calmness. Calmly set her in her crib, calmly close the door, and calmly return when the time-out is over. Other times, in the midst of a tantrum, I know Therese needs to be held. Even when she is furiously pushing me away, I can just sense her need to be in my arms and feel my calm.

You may not think there is anything catechetical about a moment such as a temper tantrum—but there is. We live in a fallen, broken world. We experience moments of pain, endure hurtful comments, and are bombarded with messages that convince us we are loved. Consequently, it only makes sense that your little one responds to the ups and downs of life with the occasional meltdown, and that we are tempted to respond with a meltdown of our own. But, by responding in a calm and loving way to our child (be that through a quieting time-out period or a soothing embrace), we teach them that there is another way to respond to the evil they face in the world. Today that "evil" may just be in the form of the toddler who took away the toy that our toddler was playing with in the sandbox, or in Mommy's refusal to give just one more cookie. But, as our little ones grow older, they will be faced with far greater evils and injustices—real and deeply rooted evils and injustices. Right now, we have the opportunity to lay the foundation for how they will respond in the future. By learning to respond to frustrations in a calm way now, they are less likely to respond in anger or unkindness later.

Let's Play!

When you set the stage, your child can thrive in an environment where she can grow in faith. Much of this growth will occur through activities and through playing with toys that aren't expressly intended for the purpose of faith formation. However, with a little creativity, some of their toys can teach them about their faith, too! Some of the religious objects you already own are quite safe for your children to play with and can be used to teach them as well.

Amy shares:

Some of Charlie's favorite "toys" were religious items of our own that he continuously pointed to or observed. We eventually realized they were safe for him to hold and decided to let him interact with them. For example, he loves carrying around a wooden crucifix we have, which is great for working on learning the word "Jesus." Many icons are printed on wooden blocks and are safe for a child to hold. One morning, while we were snuggling in bed, Charlie eyed my icon of Our Lady of Czestochowa on my nightstand and started holding it. It's only a few inches on each side; perfect for his little hands. It looks very similar to another icon we have in our dining room of the Madonna and Child. This is the icon that we have frequently held him in front of in an effort to familiarize him with the Christ child and to teach him the word "Jesus." Charlie immediately found this icon and started holding the Our Lady of Czestochowa icon up in the air to compare them. Not only was it adorable, it showed a real developmental stride in his ability to identify both Jesus and a category of objects. He spent quite a few minutes trying to hang his little icon on the wall underneath the "grown-up" icon.

In addition to making use of the objects you already have in your home, there are some religious toys available for purchase at local Catholic bookstores and online. Etsy.com is a wonderful resource for this (simply search for "Catholic toys" or something similar). Don't be afraid to think outside of the box, either. For example, buy a secondhand nativity set at less cost and allow your child to play with it (even when it is not Christmastime) in order to act out the story of Christmas and other stories from Jesus' babyhood. You can also often find holy cards and plastic statues at most Catholic bookstores. Both of these are baby/toddler-proof (be sure to get something big enough to not be a choking hazard, if your child is very small) and your little one will love playing with them!

Alternately, you can easily and inexpensively "make" your own Catholic toys, like the flannel board found **on page 110** of this book.

Prayer Corner

Children love role-playing different activities as they learn how to do new things. Consider bringing their favorite stuffed animal or doll to come and "pray" with the rest of the family during family prayer time. You can even "pretend" the doll or animal is praying by folding its hands. This personalizes the activity for your children, helping them to see that everything—even Teddy—can point us to God in some small way. Your children will love this and want to imitate the motions of their stuffed friend, which is a good first step in learning how to pray with the family.

A Wealth of Prayers

Blessing

A wonderful way to send your child off when you must separate is by blessing your child. You can also bless your child at other times—in the morning, at night, before special events, during an illness, etc. Scripture teaches us that "a father's blessing gives a family firm roots" (Sirach 3:9) and there are many instances of parents blessing their children both in Scriptures and in the lives of the saints. Your blessing may be a specific prayer you like to say each time, words of spontaneous prayer, or a simple gesture of blessing. Some of these gestures include tracing the sign of the cross on your child's forehead, placing your hands on your child, and blessing them with holy water (also with the sign of the cross). Here are some example blessings you can use:

Amy blesses Charlie, making the sign of the cross on his forehead, in the name of the Father, Son, and Holy Spirit.

> *Dear God, please bless* (name) *and help him/her to have a good day.*
>
> *May you have a good day, may God be with you in your way, and may his angel accompany you (see Tobit 5:21).*
>
> *I bless you in the name of the Father, and the Son, and the Holy Spirit.*
>
> *May the Lord bless you and keep you. May his face shine upon you. May he be gracious to you, look upon you kindly, and give you peace (see Numbers 6:24–26).*

Traveling Prayer

After you pick up your child from daycare—or anytime you travel with your child—start off the trip with a traveling prayer. You can make up a prayer on the spot, say some traditional prayers, or say the following prayer:

Guardian angel, never leave my side!
Watch over me, be my guide,
Defend me in danger, be with me in peril,
Guard my body and protect my soul.
Stay with me through this journey,
And lead me safely home.

Divine Praises

During those situations when you find yourself frustrated and need to calm down, the Divine Praises are rhythmic and soothing and easy to memorize. Their content helps us to refocus on Christ. Say them aloud to calm your child at the same time, or pray them silently to have a quieter moment with God.

Blessed be God.
Blessed be His holy name.
Blessed be Jesus Christ, true God and true man.
Blessed be the name of Jesus.
Blessed be His most Sacred Heart.
Blessed be His most precious Blood.
Blessed be Jesus in the Most Holy Sacrament of the Altar.
Blessed be the Holy Spirit, the Paraclete.
Blessed be the great Mother of God, Mary most holy.
Blessed be her holy and Immaculate Conception.
Blessed be her glorious Assumption.
Blessed be the name of Mary, Virgin and Mother.

Blessed be Saint Joseph, her most chaste spouse.
Blessed be God in His angels and in His Saints.

Offering Up Your Suffering

In Catholic tradition, we often hear the phrase "offer it up." Christ suffered on the cross and understands our suffering. By partaking in this human experience himself, he fully understands the difficulties we face and takes them onto his shoulders for us. Here are some prayers you can use to offer up your suffering:

Dear Lord, I offer you this moment for the salvation
of souls, especially that of my child.

Lord, you suffered and died for my sake
I ask you to take my suffering and redeem it.
I offer up to you all my negative thoughts and feelings
And ask you to transform them into actions of generosity.

Mary, you know a mother's joy
You know the sweet happiness of holding your child
in your arms
You also know a mother's sorrow
And the heartbreak of missing your child
During this time of sadness, pray for me and for my child
Watch over (name of your child) *on my behalf*
And entrust us to the heart of your son, Jesus. Amen.

Activities

ACTIVITY: *BIBLE FLANNEL BOARD*

You'll need:

- a bulletin board (any size)
- a large piece of flannel
- stapler or staple gun
- various pieces of felt
  (sticky-backed or nonsticky-backed)
- scissors
- glue or a glue gun

1. Begin by making your flannel board. Cover your bulletin board with your large piece of flannel and secure with staples. Trim your flannel as needed. (Alternately, you may buy a felt or flannel board online or at a teacher supply or craft store.)

2. Using your felt, you can cut out any number of shapes to represent Bible stories, objects found in church, sacraments, etc. You do not need be "crafty" to do this, for you can simply cut out shapes in the felt (using the glue to attach details), such as people, an ark, a tree (for the story of Adam and Eve), a cross, etc.

If you are not particularly crafty (or if time is an issue) you can print out images of your stories from picture Bibles or coloring pages online. You can then laminate them (with your own laminator or by having it done inexpensively at a print shop) and attach your felt to the back of your laminated images using a glue gun.

3. Once you have prepared your pictures, shapes, characters, etc., put them all in a basket and set the basket by the felt board. Sit down with your child and tell her whatever story you have prepared. Once she acts it out with you a few times she will most likely want to act it out on her own, too, so be sure to leave the felt board and pieces in a place she can easily access.

4. You can make other sets for your child to play with on her flannel board. Why not make an altar set, or a church set, or maybe even a saint set (by gluing felt to the back of your holy cards)? The possibilities are endless!

For the Record

My baby/toddler's favorite religious image to look at is _____

_____

_____

_____

Some of the toys my child played with include _____

_____

_____

_____

_____

_____

_____

Some of the Bible stories that we acted out with toys are ____

_____

_____

_____

Some of my child's favorite saints and Bible characters include

_____

_____

_____

We bless our little one with the following prayer: _____

_____

_____

_____

_____

_____

Chapter 6

THE LITURGICAL YEAR IN THE HOME

As families, we are familiar with celebrating. We celebrate birthdays, holidays, first and last days of school, graduations, and everything in between. Your family may celebrate special days by going out for dinner, or eating cake, or giving presents. There is a rhythm to our family celebrations and a rhythm to when we celebrate what we do throughout the year.

The Church family has a similar rhythm, much of it similar to our family rhythm. The Church's rhythm of celebrations and memorials is called the liturgical year. As a family, you can celebrate these special feasts along with the Church.

About the Liturgical Year

Did you know that **Advent** is actually the beginning of the liturgical year? Common guesses include dates such as Christmas or Easter, but it is actually the first Sunday in Advent. According to the *General Norms for the Liturgical Year,* "Advent has a twofold character: as a season to prepare for Christmas when Christ's first coming to us is remembered; as a season when that remembrance directs the mind and heart to await Christ's Second Coming at the end of time" (from No. 39, *General Norms for the Liturgical Year and the Calendar,* by the Congregation for Divine Worship. February 14, 1969.

Accessed through http://www.ewtn.com/library/CURIA/
CDWLITYR.HTM).

Many of us acknowledge that Advent prepares our hearts
to welcome Jesus as we recall Christ's first coming (Christmas), but Advent is actually preparing us for Christ's Second
Coming at the end of time. Advent means "coming," and as
Jesus already came about 2,000 years ago, Christians await in
"joyful hope" the Second Coming of Christ our risen Lord.

The season immediately following Advent in the liturgical
calendar year is **Christmas**. The Christmas season begins with
evening prayer on Christmas Eve and ends on the Sunday
after Epiphany, or after January 6. Next to Easter, "the Church
holds most sacred the memorial of Christ's birth and early
manifestations" (*General Norms*, No. 32). During the Scripture
readings, we hear tales of John the Baptist proclaiming Jesus'
coming, Mary visiting Elizabeth while pregnant, and Jesus
preaching about the Second Coming. This is a time for great
celebration, as we recall Christ's first coming and continue to
look forward to his next and final coming. Some of the rich-
est family traditions often revolve around this time of year,
usually a very joyful time.

Ordinary time is interspersed throughout the liturgical year between our moments of fasting and celebrations
(feasts). Though this season is called "ordinary," it is essential to remember that our faith is always extraordinary. We
need ordinary time in order to deepen our understanding
of the extraordinary events that take place within our faith
life. Ordinary time in the liturgical year takes place between
Christmas and Lent, and from Pentecost to the feast of Christ
the King (the Sunday before the first Sunday of Advent). Did
you know that many feasts take place within ordinary time?

For example, every Sunday is considered a feast day for the Church. We also celebrate many feast days for saints, Marian feasts, the exaltation of the cross, etc.

Lent is a forty-day journey in which we prepare for the celebration of Easter. It contains a number of special liturgies. The season begins with Ash Wednesday and culminates in the celebration of Holy Week, which "has as its purpose the remembrance of Christ's passion, beginning with his Messianic entrance into Jerusalem" (*General Norms,* No. 31). Lent is a solemn season of fasting, prayer, and almsgiving, where we focus on Christ's suffering and ask our risen Lord to assist us as we prepare our hearts for Easter. Very small children typically cannot give alms in the traditional sense (although it may be a good time of year to give away toys and clothes that are not being used), so are not required to fast in the same way as adults. We can help them to "fast" in other ways. For example, we might put away some of their toys for the season and bring out more faith-based activities and religious objects instead. Most importantly, we can practice an increased devotion to prayer with our children during Lent.

The **Easter Triduum** begins with the evening Mass of the Lord's Supper on Holy Thursday (Thursday night Mass, known commonly by the washing of the feet), includes Good Friday and Holy Saturday, and closes with Evening Prayer on Easter. These few days are burgeoning with rich liturgical celebrations at all times of the day, giving you ample opportunity to attend some with your family. This time is extremely important, and the Church teaches us that "the Easter Triduum of the passion and resurrection of Christ is the culmination of the entire liturgical year" (*General Norms,* No. 18).

The **Easter** season begins with the celebration of Easter (beginning on Holy Saturday at the Easter Vigil) and ends with **Pentecost**, a total of fifty days. The Alleluia makes its joyful return to the Mass after taking a leave of absence during Lent. During this time, we continue to celebrate the resurrection of Christ even after Easter has ended.

When we think about Advent, Christmas, Lent, and Easter, there are special foods, customs, decorations, and actions we can associate with them. However, when we think about ordinary time, it is so easy to think about it as filler space, or a time between the special seasons. How can one celebrate ordinary time? In a sense, there is nothing particularly extraordinary about this time. And that in itself is important, too—it is a resting period of sorts that helps us to see more clearly the extraordinary realities of our faith. The simplicity of ordinary time helps us to become more acutely aware of the tremendous beauty found in other seasons—and even throughout the ordinary.

Celebrating the Seasons With a Little One

There are so many different calendars and seasons in today's world that we mark our lives around: fall, winter, spring, and summer; tax season; Christmas shopping season; the school year and summer break; a busy or slow season at work; wedding season; etc. But the most important seasons in our lives—the liturgical seasons—are often overlooked in our busyness. These seasons should set the tone for our prayer lives, quiet musings, and day-to-day living. Unfortunately, it is all too easy to notice the differences while at church and forget about the season we are in until the next Sunday rolls around. Your challenge is to fight this complacency by working the season into your family's life at home in a way that affects even your youngest members.

Visuals such as decorations and activities are some of the most effective ways to communicate a change of season to your children. Special prayers are also extremely important parts of our Catholic tradition when celebrating different liturgical seasons. Continue to follow some of the ideas suggested in the chapter on prayer with some of the prayer ideas listed in this chapter.

Infants

While even the subtlest of visual cues can remind an adult that a new liturgical season is upon us, your newborn will have little awareness that something new is going on, as everything is new to him or her. Instead of trying to teach an infant what each liturgical season is, you can simply immerse your youngest child in any special seasonal activities. As much as you can, include your child in all your family activities, such as special prayers, decorating the house, and attending special seasonal liturgies. He may not fully understand what he is participating in, but there is still every reason to include him as much as possible, as he is a full member of your family (and of the Church family if baptized). It is important for older siblings and you as parents to grow accustomed to including them so it is already second nature when they are old enough to understand.

Your older infant interacts with the world more actively and enjoys manipulating items with her hands. Encourage her to interact with traditional decorations by picking them up and looking at them. Be sure to have child-safe versions of decorations so your infant can fully investigate them. Let's look at Advent as an example. One such traditional decoration is a nativity scene—perfect for tiny hands. If she is trying to talk, be sure to describe to her what she is holding and repeat important names, such as "Mary" and "Jesus." You could even pray to the Holy Family or say an Advent prayer every time she interacts with the nativity scene. Some other options include Jesse Tree ornaments during Advent (symbols from the line of Jesse found in Scripture), angel or infant Jesus dolls/figurines for Christmas, a crucifix during Lent, and a risen Jesus icon for Easter. Items appropriate during all times of the year can be focused on during ordinary time such as rosaries, figurines of the disciples, and holy cards. These objects can be both interactive and prayerful in nature, meeting your child at her level of understanding.

Toddlers

At this age, your child will more easily notice differences in decorations and routine activities. Take advantage of this. These will be your greatest tools for teaching her about the different seasons at a young age. These are prime years for learning language, and your child can understand much more than she can put into words. As much as possible, talk to her about new decorations and describe what you are doing and why you are doing it. For example, when you place a star on the top of your Christmas tree, try to teach her the word "star." Then show her a nativity scene or a nativity painting with the Bethlehem star and repeat the word "star." Take the hook out of a star ornament and allow her to hold it in her hands and look over the object.

When adding special seasonal prayers to your normal routine, explain ahead of time to your toddler that you are starting a new and special prayer. Use the name of the liturgical season frequently to help him associate these new prayers, activities, and decorations with a central theme. Tell him that the decoration is a Christmas star, sing Christmas songs with him, and explain that you will be learning a new Christmas prayer.

Have special toys that you designate for each liturgical season. These may be themed (such as animals found at the birth of Christ for Advent) or colored (put out a basket of green toys each time ordinary season comes around). You may also wish to take advantage of an older toddler's increasing interest in colors and highlight the colors of each liturgical season to you children. Point out the color of the priest's vestments at Mass, and use colored cloths on your prayer table. Say the name of the color and the season over and over ("Look at the green

> *Ordinary time = green*
> *Christmas/Easter = white*
> *Advent/Lent = purple*
> *Triduum/Pentecost = red*

for ordinary time. So much green! Can you find the green?") These interactions may seem silly now, but you are laying the groundwork for later catechesis.

Preschoolers

Discussions with your children are now very important for their learning. Before, they were learning the most basic forms of communication, and now they may be constantly pestering you with questions. Where does the sun go at night? Why do birds sing? What is this for? These questions are great opportunities for you to jump in and instruct. Try to have as many conversations with them about the faith as possible. Whenever they have a question, answer as best as you can and encourage them to ask you more questions. Find ways to prompt questioning. Continue to have special toys for each liturgical season—this will surely prompt questions. They will most likely ask why there are new toys, and if you give them a group of toys colored according to the liturgical season, they will ask you why they are all a certain color. If you are having trouble explaining the change in seasons to them, compare the church seasons to the calendar seasons. Outside, the air gets colder or warmer when the seasons change. The plants look different, and the trees change colors. Snow may even fall. Inside, we also change things around us. We change the decorations and the colors to remind us what season it is. The colors help us to relate to the season. These seasons are very special and help us to remember Jesus' life on earth. Continue to help your children learn what seasons the different colors indicate. Coloring sheets can also help in this venture, and a simple online search can yield a number of free ones as well.

At this age, your children are full-fledged participants in family activities—think about how far they've come since infancy. By now, you are hopefully used to including your young ones in all activities and helping them to find their own special way to participate. At this age, preschoolers want to be like the "big people" and they love to mimic our actions. When performing new season-themed activities, focus on specific actions they will be able to mimic. For example, many versions of the Stations of the Cross involve genuflecting. Help your children to genuflect toward the crucifix at the appropriate time, and perhaps whisper to them "kneel for Jesus." It can be difficult for children to pay attention for an entire liturgical celebration such as this, but having one activity for them to focus on draws their attention to God in that moment. They can also help you open a window on the Advent calendar, venerate the cross with a kiss, or read the Bible by your side. The more you perform these actions, the more your child will. Leading by example is one of the best ways to teach a young child.

Just as they follow your lead, follow your child's lead to see what interests him. Rituals, customs, and traditions surrounding the liturgical seasons should be introduced to your child with careful explanation and example. After the first time or two performing a custom, suggest part of that custom your child might carry out. For example, you might say, "It's your turn to put an ornament on the Jesse Tree tonight. Where would you like to put it?" After some time of encouragement, you can be more open-ended with your preschooler, especially if he is more adventurous. Once he is familiar with the activity, ask him, "What part of Lenten prayer would you like to do tonight?" If he is too timid to claim something to do on his own, return to offering a gentle suggestion, but keep asking him how he would like to participate. Eventually he may feel comfortable enough with the new activity to choose a part he enjoys doing. By allowing your child to carry out the task of his choice, you are encouraging ownership of that action.

Preschoolers notoriously love being included in experiences. Hopefully, this will help him to pay better attention. For example, during Lenten prayer, you may suggest that he start the prayer time for everyone by making the sign of the cross, or you may prompt your child to begin intercessory or free-form prayer time (some older toddlers may be able to do this, too). After some time, he may decide to choose on his own what part of prayer he would like to contribute. Children are creative, so don't be surprised if they pick something you would never think of—like holding the prayer book.

Prayer Corner

Hopefully by now you have been able to set up a family prayer corner. This is a great place to implement some obvious changes with the turning of each Church season. One of the simplest ways to bring the liturgical year into your home is through decoration. Even when you forget that a new season has begun in the Church's calendar year, you are reminded very quickly when you walk into the sanctuary and notice new banners, the presence (or absence) of plants and flowers, and different colored vestments worn by the priest. There is no reason to believe that these changes should stop at the church door. If your child wakes up one day and sees that the prayer corner looks vastly different, you have already accomplished some basic communication about the different time that has been entered.

If your child is very young, simply be sure to change the decorations the night before the new season begins, after prayer time is over. When your child is starting to talk, teach her the name of these new objects. Help her to learn that they are associated with that part of the Liturgical year (that is, Advent candles, Easter lilies, etc.). This will help your little one differentiate these objects as holding special meaning for different seasons (that is, not all candles are Advent candles, and we only use Advent candles during Advent). If your child is older, discuss with her the meaning of these objects and ask for her help arranging or even purchasing/making these objects. The items will hold more importance if the child is involved from step one. For special seasons, you may wish to incorporate your new decorations in and around your regular decorations, or you may wish to put your ordinary items away only during that period of time. These decorations can be incorporated easily into your prayer corner, but do not stop there. You can also choose to make relatively minor changes to your prayer corner and focus on using some of these decorations in other places in your home, or you can use them in multiple places. The suggestions in this chapter are simply that—suggestions. Use them as a springboard of ideas that can be creatively adjusted to fit the needs and desires of your own family.

Advent

Decorate with Advent candles (unlit or at a safe distance), an Advent wreath or some simple greenery, an empty manger or even a complete nativity scene ready for baby Jesus and his parents, a star of Bethlehem; purple and rose linens/decorations (the rose linens are for *Gaudete* [Rejoice] Sunday, the third Sunday of Advent), an Advent calendar.

Christmas

Remove your Advent candles—it's a new season. Consider adding different candles, such as white, gold, or silver ones. Place Jesus, Mary, and Joseph in the nativity scene and one or many angels to declare Jesus' entry into the world. Use white linens at this time (or Christmas linens if you have them available). During the Christmas season, your decor should be fancier than during Advent, since this is the fulfillment of those anticipations. A painting of the nativity scene and your completed Jesse tree may also grace your prayer corner. Enjoy celebrating Christmas counterculturally by beginning your celebration on the twenty-fifth of December and ending on the Sunday after Epiphany.

Lent

Keep an overall simple feel, perhaps even take away (or cover with a cloth) some of the ordinary decorations or items you have in order to focus on just a few. Be certain to include a crucifix during this time if you don't ordinarily have one. You may also want to place your palms from Palm Sunday into your prayer corner. Some like to incorporate desert-like décor to remind us of Jesus' forty days spent in the desert. Use purple linens throughout Lent and red linens on Good Friday.

Easter

While Christmas is a kind of continuation of Advent, Easter should stand in stark contrast to Lent, since the resurrection was such a surprising miracle. White, silver, and gold decorations set a tone of jubilation. Typically we see a lot more greenery and plants during this season to indicate the new life we are given in Christ. Consider placing an Easter lily plant and an icon of the Sacred Heart of Jesus or the resurrected Christ in your prayer corner at this time.

Ordinary time

Leave your prayer corner as you would normally. You may want to consider an injection of green, since this is the color of ordinary time. Holy cards with different images and prayers are also a lovely addition to the ordinary time prayer table. Though the time is ordinary, the life in God is still extraordinary. Consider reflecting the seasons of the year by decorating with flowers to adorn this prayer space that will change from winter through fall.

A Wealth of Prayers

Advent and Christmas carols

Choose from a large variety of hymns and religious carols to use during some of your prayer times. Singing is a beautiful form of prayer and soothes little ones. Setting words to music can also make it much easier for the older children to remember and pray along with these words. Singing to them during prayer time also helps your children to understand the true purpose of these carols, which can get lost when they are overplayed on the radio or during nonreligious events. Make sure you are using songs during the correct season—some hymns are best suited for only Advent or Christmas, depending on the content.

Some suggested hymns for Advent:

"Come, O Long Expected Jesus"

O Antiphons (Advent)—From December 17–24 we remember the special names and titles given to Jesus. During this time you could sing appropriate verses of "O Come, O Come Emmanuel" on each day, such as "O Come, O Come, O...Wisdom, Leader, Flower, Key, Radiant Dawn, King, Emmanuel, etc."

Some suggested hymns for Christmas:

"What Child Is This?"

"O Come, All Ye Faithful"

"O Little Town of Bethlehem"

"Silent Night"

"Away in a Manger"

"Lo, How a Rose E'er Blooming"

Lent

The Chaplet of Divine Mercy—This traditional prayer is prayed using a rosary but is much faster than the rosary and great for short attention spans. Saint Faustina was gifted this form of prayer in beautiful visions she had of Jesus. Its focus on Jesus' suffering and passion makes it especially fitting for Lent, though it is a wonderful prayer to use throughout all the liturgical seasons. The other emphasis of this prayer is God's infinite love and mercy, and it is a great way to teach your little one about God's love that is literally "pouring out of his heart" for them (using the Divine Mercy image, which can be found online, is a fantastic way to illustrate this).

Easter/paschal greeting

On Easter and during Easter season, your priest may use the paschal greeting. Its use during the liturgical year is limited and so is a very obvious mark of the Easter season. Use it during the Easter season in front of your infant or young child to expose him to this beautiful greeting. Help your talking children to say some of the words or to entirely learn the greeting. It may be helpful if one parent always says the greeting, while the other parent and children always say the response. There are many forms of this greeting, so perhaps choose one for your family to use.

Greeting: Christ is risen!
Response: Truly he is risen!
Greeting: Christ is risen!
Response: Indeed, he is risen!
Greeting: He is risen!
Response: He is risen indeed! Alleluia, alleluia!

Ordinary time

Continue on with your regular prayer routine! As mentioned earlier, the simplicity of ordinary time is part of what makes the other seasons feel so rich. If desired, find a Catholic calendar that lists the feast days throughout the year. Many saints have a feast day, and most days of the year celebrate a specific saint. During one of your prayer times (or all of them!) during the day, say a short prayer asking for their intercession (for example, "Saint Athanasius, pray for us!"). On the feast day of your child's special patron saint (the saint associated with her name), consider having a special celebration to commemorate that day.

Activities

ACTIVITY 1: *JESSE TREE* (ADVENT)

The **Jesse Tree** is a special tradition that helps the family to consider the "family tree" of Jesus. By praying the Jesse Tree, you will read the Scriptures leading up to the birth of Christ while looking at images related to each story (such as an apple for Adam and Eve, an ark for Noah, etc.)

You will need:
- Jesse Tree printouts
- String or yarn
- A small Christmas tree

1. Begin by doing a simple Internet search for "Jesse Tree" or "Make Your Own Jesse Tree." You should be able to find a set that you can print out, complete with corresponding Scripture verses.

2. Print out the paper ornaments and cut them out. You can simply punch a hole in the top of each ornament and put a loop of string or yarn through it. If you have the time, you or your children can color the ornaments and you can mount them to card stock or laminate them for durability.

3. Each night during family prayer time, read the corresponding story from Scripture and hang up the ornament (on your small Christmas tree or on your full-sized tree) for that night.

ACTIVITY 2: *SET UP A NATIVITY SCENE* (CHRISTMAS)

Most families have a nativity scene, and if you do not yet have one, now would be a good time to get one. If possible, select one that is durable and unbreakable. If you have one that is breakable, allow your child to play with it and handle it with your supervision. Either way, find some way for your little one to interact with these special objects.

You will need:

- Your family nativity scene

1. Begin by talking to your child as you unpack the nativity scene from its box. Say, "Oh, what is this? This is something special. This is our nativity scene. Do you want to help me set it up?"

2. As you unpack each figure in the nativity, ask your child if he knows the name of it. If he is very young, you can simply name each figure as you unpack it. After you name it, let your little one handle it.

3. Once all the figures are unpacked, set up the nativity scene together, talking about the Christmas story as you do.

ACTIVITY 3: *DESERT SENSORY BIN (LENT)*

You will need:

- Small bag of play sand
- Plastic bin or large shoebox
- Small wooden cross or crosses
- Small rocks (use your judgment, based on your child)
- Small sticks or wooden log blocks (or plain blocks)
- Any animal toys you may have that would be found in the desert

1. Pour the play sand into your box and arrange your desert objects inside.

2. Tell your child the story of Jesus in the desert: "Jesus once went to the desert to pray for forty days and forty nights. During Lent, we spend forty days praying in a special way so we may be closer to Jesus."

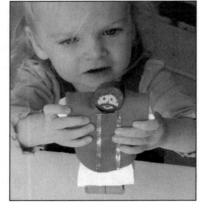

Therese interacts curiously with a figurine of Jesus.

3. Talk to your child about the desert. Is it dry or wet? Is it green or brown? Do lots of people and animals live there or not? Talk with him about how Lent is our time in the desert: "Just as the desert is dry and empty, we make our lives dry by fasting (refraining from our celebrations) during Lent. We empty our lives of extra things so we can get to know Jesus better." If your child does not know the answers to these questions, consider incorporating some picture books that take

place in the desert, or show him pictures of the desert during his normal play time.

4. After this introduction, leave the sensory bin out for your little one to play with.

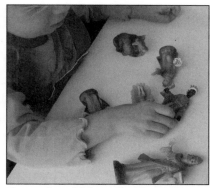

Therese plays with figures from a nativity set.

ACTIVITY 4: *MAKE YOUR OWN PASCHAL CANDLE* (EASTER)

One key feature of the Easter Vigil service is the blessing of your parish's tall and beautiful paschal candle, which will remain lit all throughout the Easter season. Some families like to make their own small version of this candle to light on their dinner tables or prayer tables during the Easter season. Take a picture of your parish's candle or do an Internet search for examples for this activity.

You will need:

- White pillar candle
- Acrylic paint or a paschal candle kit (which can be purchased online)
- Whole cloves

1. If desired, paint your pillar candle so that it looks like the pictures of paschal candles that you have found (it can be left plain as well). You may also wish to place cloves on each point of the cross, similar to the incense pieces that are placed in the real paschal candle.

2. Once you have decorated your candle, place it either on your prayer table or family dinner table. Explain it to your child, using the image of "Christ our light." Also teach her the word "paschal" and explain that it is another way to say "Easter": "Do you see this special candle? It is like the candle at church, the paschal candle. Paschal is another word for Easter. This candle reminds us that Jesus is our light. Just like the candle lights up this room, Jesus lights up our lives."

3. Light the candle each evening, either while you pray together or eat your meals.

ACTIVITY 5: *LITURGICAL COLOR SENSORY BIN* (ORDINARY TIME)

Every season of the Church year has its own color. This activity will help your little one to learn the colors of the liturgical year.

You will need:

- Plastic bin or large shoebox
- Colored objects (all green, all red, all white, or all purple)

1. Fill up your bin with colored objects that are the same color as the liturgical season.

2. When you introduce the bin to your child, talk to him about the color of the items in the bin and connect it to the liturgical season: "What color are the objects in the bin? Are they green? They are green like the color we see in ordinary time. It is ordinary time." The bin will serve as a reminder of what season you are celebrating. Note: The objects do not need to be religious objects, they just need to be the color of the corresponding Church season.

3. Once you've introduced your child to this bin, leave it out for ongoing play.

ACTIVITY 6: *PATRON SAINT DAY PARTY* (ORDINARY TIME)

There is a special saint associated with almost every day of the liturgical year. A simple online search can help you determine what day is the feast day of your child's patron saint (the saint associated with his or her name or the saint that is special to your child and family).

You will need:

- Party supplies/decorations
- Cake or special dessert

1. When your child's patron saint day arrives, start the day by wishing him or her:

   "Happy _____ Day!

   _____ is your patron saint."

   Keep telling her this throughout the day.

2. You may wish to do special things with your child on this day (take her to daily Mass, go on a special trip to the park or zoo, etc.).

3. Make a cake or buy a special dessert to have with lunch or dinner. You may wish to decorate if you have the time: hanging up streamers, using a special tablecloth, lighting candles, etc. Tell your whole family that these special decorations are to celebrate (child's name) patron saint day!

4. At dinner, talk about the life of your child's patron saint and enjoy your special dessert!

For the Record

The first Christmas carol I sang was _____

_____

I first attended midnight Mass on _____

_____

I first went to the Liturgies of the Triduum on _____

_____

_____

_____

_____

_____

When I was little, my favorite time of the Church year was

_____

_____

_____

Here's a funny or cute story from my family's prayer time

together: _____

_____

_____

_____

_____

_____

_____

_____

_____

Conclusion

BABY STEPS OF FAITH

One of the most precious moments for a parent is seeing her child take her first steps. The hesitation, the unsteadiness, and the joy on her face when she sees she is capable of walking is so beautiful. Our steps on the journey of faith with our little ones are no different. God knows we are apprehensive about the task of raising our children in the faith. He knows our first steps in this direction may be unsteady ones and that we may not do this task perfectly.

And yet this journey of faith is what God asks of us as parents. Each parent deals with moments of insecurity, moments of questioning the ability to parent well, but God has given you the child (or children) he has for a reason. He has given you your little ones knowing full well what your gifts are, what your weaknesses are, and knowing that you are the one who can best meet the needs of your child. Whether your child is biologically yours, adopted by you, or even if you are currently fostering a little one, God has entrusted this child to you specifically because he knows you and your gifts and talents. God knows that you are the one best suited to lead this little one closer to him.

We hope you are encouraged after reading this book and feel empowered to begin (or continue) teaching your littlest one about the Catholic faith. We also hope you are excited by any new ideas you've read in this book and look forward to implementing them. But what if you're just feeling...overwhelmed?

If you feel overwhelmed—and the best of parents do—take inspiration from your baby. Think of those baby steps. Don't be afraid to make your own uncertain steps, trusting in your Father in heaven, knowing that he—a parent who loves you even more than you love your child—will be there to hold you up. You don't have to do this perfectly. Rely on God's grace to help you and enjoy the beauty of this journey of faith with your child.

About the Authors

Michele E. Chronister received her B.A. and M.A. degrees in theology from the University of Notre Dame. In graduate school, she had the opportunity to work with preschoolers in a catechetical setting through the "Catechesis of the Good Shepherd" program. She lives in Missouri with her husband and daughter. Visit Michele on her blog: http://welcometomydomesticmonastery. blogspot.com/.

Amy M. Garro received her B.A. in theology from the University of Notre Dame and served as a teacher in a Catholic school. During her university experience she trained and worked as an assistant teacher at a local daycare, and learned about catechizing to young children. She also completed an internship in parish youth ministry, where she was mentored to adapt catechetical programs and tools.

Introducing Children to Silence and Prayer
For Catechists and Parents

ISBN: 9780764-823145

Through prayer, very young children can learn to talk with God and to build their faith and trust in him in the greatest and hardest of times. In *Introducing Children to Silence and Prayer*, author Luis M. Benavides, explores this belief. By walking catechists and families through the process, he helps them to get to know God and to communicate with the God who loves them. Benavides also helps us reexamine our own attitudes about prayer as he offers a different perspective to help children begin the journey and deepen their relationship with God.

Handbook for Today's Catholic Children

ISBN: 9780764-810138

Written for younger children, *Handbook for Today's Catholic Children* presents basic tenets of the Catholic faith in terms they can understand. Chapter topics include "All About Sin—More About Love," and "The Church Cares for You," which discusses the Ten Commandments. Each chapter ends with a short prayer.

My Sister Is Annoying!
And Other Prayers for Children

ISBN: 9780764-818271

My Sister is Annoying! is a beautifully illustrated, fun way for children to talk to God about things that are important to them.